Marx Joyce
Abbott Hardy Machiavelli Chesterton Cooper Emerson Austen Grimm
Defoe Melville Montaigne Haggard Hugo
Eliot
Stoker Carroll Christie Molière
Wilde Maupassant Byron Schiller
Garnett Einstein Fitzgerald Engels Smith Kafka
Goethe Hawthorne Hall
Cotton Dostoyevsky Kipling Doyle Willis
Baum Henry Nietzsche
Leslie Dumas Flaubert Turgenev Balzac
Stockton Vatsyayana Crane
Burroughs Verne
Curtis Tocqueville Whitman Gogol Vinci
Homer Widger Tolstoy Busch
Darwin Thoreau Twain Scott Plato Harte
Potter Freud Zola Lawrence Dickens Burton Hesse
Kant Jowett Stevenson Cervantes
Andersen Voltaire Cooke
London Descartes Wells
Poe Aristotle Burton Irving
Hale James Hastings
Bunner Shakespeare
Richter Chekhov Chambers da Irving
Doré Dante Shaw Benedict Alcott
Swift Wodehouse Pushkin
Newton

tredition®

tredition was established in 2006 by Sandra Latusseck and Soenke Schulz. Based in Hamburg, Germany, tredition offers publishing solutions to authors and publishing houses, combined with world-wide distribution of printed and digital book content. tredition is uniquely positioned to enable authors and publishing houses to create books on their own terms and without conventional manufacturing risks.

For more information please visit: www.tredition.com

TREDITION CLASSICS

This book is part of the TREDITION CLASSICS series. The creators of this series are united by passion for literature and driven by the intention of making all public domain books available in printed format again - worldwide. Most TREDITION CLASSICS titles have been out of print and off the bookstore shelves for decades. At tredition we believe that a great book never goes out of style and that its value is eternal. Several mostly non-profit literature projects provide content to tredition. To support their good work, tredition donates a portion of the proceeds from each sold copy. As a reader of a TREDITION CLASSICS book, you support our mission to save many of the amazing works of world literature from oblivion. See all available books at www.tredition.com.

Project Gutenberg

The content for this book has been graciously provided by Project Gutenberg. Project Gutenberg is a non-profit organization founded by Michael Hart in 1971 at the University of Illinois. The mission of Project Gutenberg is simple: To encourage the creation and distribution of eBooks. Project Gutenberg is the first and largest collection of public domain eBooks.

The Children's Book of Celebrated Pictures

Lorinda Munson Bryant

Imprint

This book is part of TREDITION CLASSICS

Author: Lorinda Munson Bryant
Cover design: Buchgut, Berlin – Germany

Publisher: tredition GmbH, Hamburg - Germany
ISBN: 978-3-8472-1557-8

www.tredition.com
www.tredition.de

THE CHILDREN'S BOOK

OF

CELEBRATED PICTURES

BY

LORINDA MUNSON BRYANT

Author of "Famous Pictures of Real Boys and Girls," "Famous Pictures of Real Animals," etc.

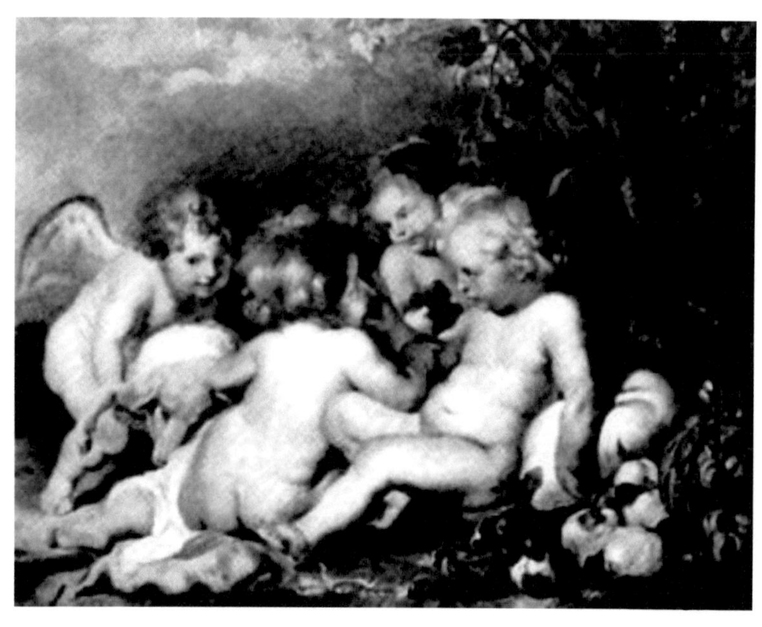

PUBLISHED BY THE CENTURY CO.

New York

Copyright, 1922, by

The Century Co.

To My Daughter

BERTHA COOKINGHAM BRYANT

Dear Children:

The stories I am telling about the pictures and their painters in this book are gathered from many countries. Some of them belong to very early times when history was told to grown up people by story-tellers at banquets and in the homes, on the street corners and public halls. Some of the stories are legends and traditions that grew up with the beginnings of the Christian era. All of them are taken from authentic sources and many of them illustrate some natural law.

The artists who painted these pictures knew history and the early myths, the fairy-tales, the legends and the traditions, the Bible and the Apocrypha. We love these pictures because they are beautiful and true, but really to understand them we must know what the artists had in mind when they painted them.

If you learn to know these pictures and love them, I will make you another book soon about statues and their stories.

With love and best wishes, from your friend,

Lorinda Munson Bryant

[2]

THE HOLY FAMILY

Bernardino Pintoricchio (1454-1513)

In looking at pictures of the old masters you will often see one called the "Holy Family." I want you to know who belonged to the Holy Family. The grown people are Joseph and Mary, the father and mother of Jesus; they had no last names at that time. The children are Jesus and his cousin, John the Baptist, six months older than Jesus. Sometimes the little John's mother, Elizabeth, is in the picture and sometimes his father, Zacharias, is there also.

In this picture painted by Pintoricchio, Jesus is about four years old and John four and a half. The Bible story gives very little about the growing up of these children. Of Jesus it says, "And the child grew, and waxed strong in spirit, filled with wisdom; and the grace of God was upon him." And of John it says, "And the child grew, and waxed strong in spirit, and he was in the deserts till the day of showing unto Israel."

One story from a very old book, "The Infancy," tells about Jesus playing with the other boys. It says:

"And when Jesus was seven years of age, he was on a certain day with other boys, his companions about the same age. Who when they were at play, made clay into several shapes, namely, asses, oxen, birds, and other figures, each boasting of his work, endeavoring to exceed the rest.

"Then the Lord Jesus said to the boys, I will command these figures which I have made to walk. And immediately they moved, and when he commanded them to return they returned. He also made figures of birds and sparrows, which, when he commanded to fly, did fly, and when he commanded to stand still, did stand still; and if he gave them meat and drink, they did eat and drink." [3]

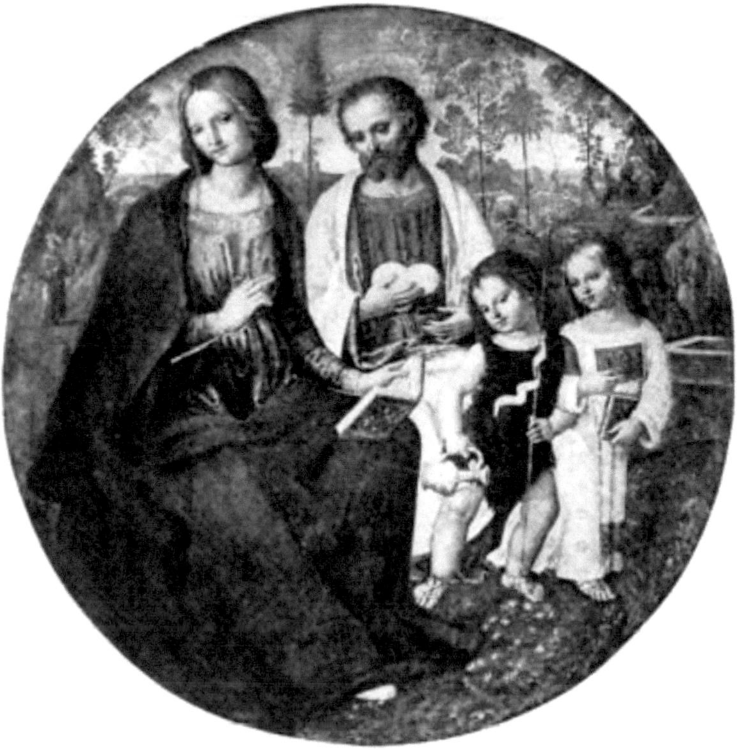

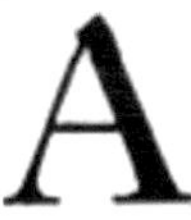

Courtesy of Pratt Institute

Fig. 1. The Holy Family. Pintoricchio. Academy, Siena

[4]

THE VALLEY FARM

John Constable (1776-1837)

A n old man, eighty-four years of age, lived in this house on "The Valley Farm," in England. He was born here and he used to say that he had never been away from this house but four days in all his life. He asked Constable to come and paint a picture of his home. And what a beautiful picture it is! The old house, snuggled down so close to the little stream, could paddle its feet—if it had any—in the cool water. And see how tenderly the tall trees keep guard over it. How we wish that we could be there too! If only we could be in the punt—I am sure it is a punt-boat even if one end of it is pointed—and be rowed up and down in the delightful shade. Those two in the boat have no doubt been for the cows and are driving them home to be milked.

John Constable liked to choose his subjects for his pictures from the familiar scenes near his home. He used to say to his friends:

"I have always succeeded best with my native scenes. They have always charmed me, and I hope they always will." [5]

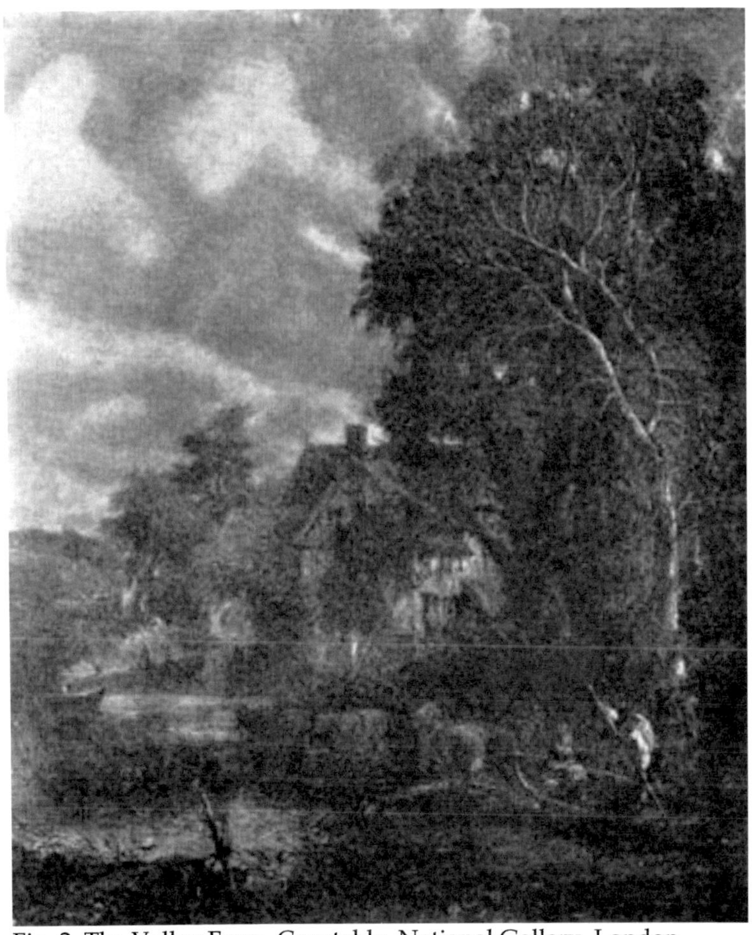

Fig. 2. The Valley Farm. Constable. National Gallery, London

[6]

THE MADONNA AND CHILD WITH
ST. JEROME

Antonio Allegri Da Correggio (1494?-1534)

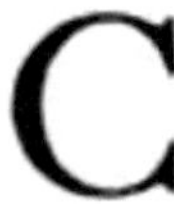

orreggio loved to paint darling babies, lovely angels, beautiful women and splendid men. In this picture of "the Madonna and St. Jerome," I want you specially to see St. Jerome and his lion. St. Jerome, a very noted man who lived four centuries after Christ, was the first person to translate the New Testament into Latin. It was called "The Vulgate," because of its common use in the Latin Church.

When St. Jerome was thirty years old he went away from the city of Rome and became a hermit and lived in desert places in the East. One day, so the story goes, as he sat at the gate of the monastery a lion came up limping as though he had been hurt. The other hermits ran away but St. Jerome went to meet the lion. The lion lifted up his paw and St. Jerome found a thorn in his foot. He took out the thorn and bound up the poor paw, so the lion stayed with St. Jerome and kept guard over an ass that brought the wood from the forest.

One day when the lion was asleep a caravan of merchants came along and stole the ass. The poor ashamed lion hung his head before the saint, and Jerome thought he had killed and eaten the ass. To punish him St. Jerome had him do the work of the ass and bring the wood from the forest. One day some time afterward the lion saw the ass coming down the road leading a caravan of camels. The Arabs often have an ass lead the camels. The lion knew that it was the stolen ass, so he led the caravan into the convent grounds. The merchant found that he was caught. St. Jerome was very glad to find that his lion was honest and true. Whenever you see a picture of a saint with a lion you must remember that it is St. Jerome, the great Latin scholar. [7]

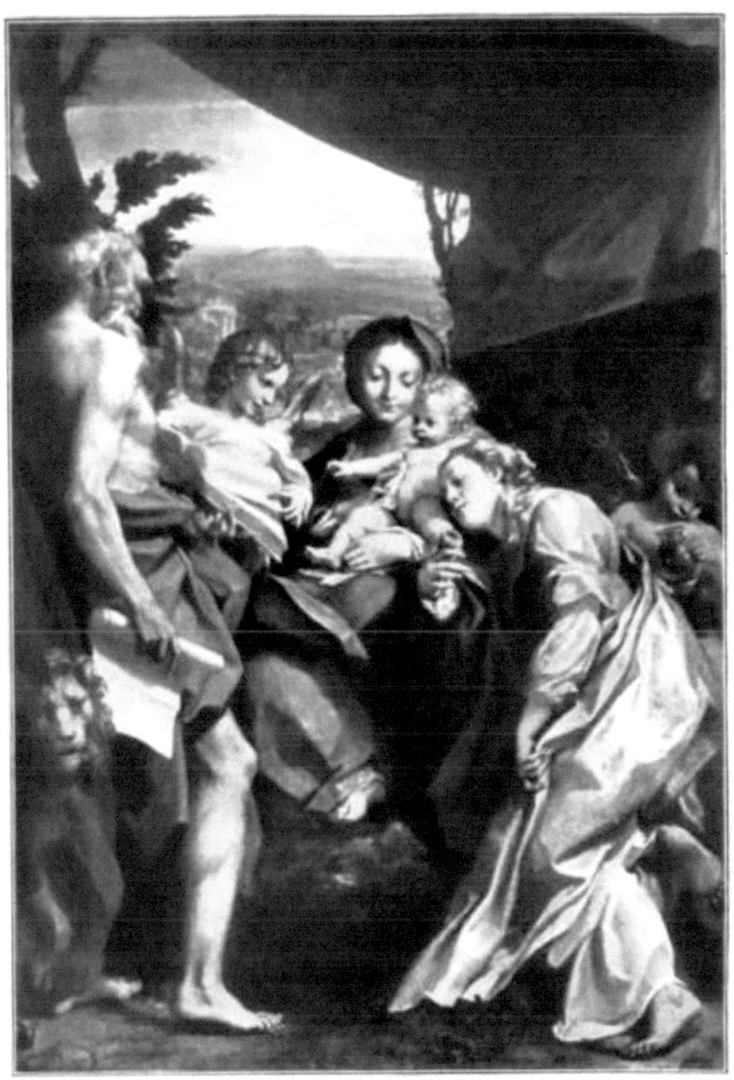

Courtesy of Pratt Institute

Fig. 3. Madonna and St. Jerome. Correggio. Parma Gallery, Italy
[8]

THE WOOD GATHERERS

Jean Baptiste Camille Corot (1796-1875)

The picture of "The Wood Gatherers" is very precious to us. It is the last picture Corot signed after he was confined to the bed, a few days before he died.

A curious story is told of Corot's painting this picture. He had an old study of another artist's of a landscape with St. Jerome at prayer: you remember I told you the story of St. Jerome and his lion. Corot took the study and made a number of sketches of it. Somehow his landscape would not fit St. Jerome, so he painted a man on horseback and a dog going off into the woods. Then in the place of St. Jerome praying he put a woman gathering bits of wood and another woman with a bundle of fagots under her arm. Now the picture must have another name and he called it "The Wood Gatherers." When you go to Washington, you must not fail to see this picture in the Corcoran Art Gallery. [9]

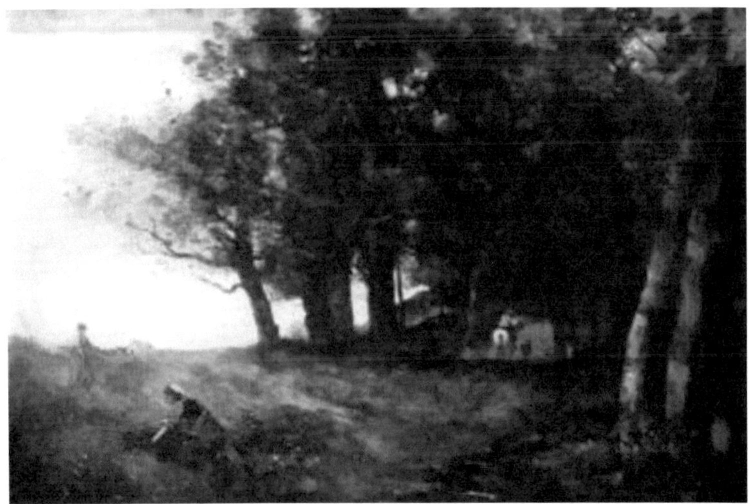

Fig. 4. The Wood-Gatherers. Corot. Courtesy of the Corcoran Art
Gallery, Washington, D. C.

[10]

AURORA

Guido Reni (1575-1642)

Hyperion had three wonderful children, Apollo, the god of the sun,
Selene, the goddess of the moon, and Aurora, the goddess of the
dawn. When Aurora appears her sister, Selene (the moon), fades
and night rolls back like a curtain. Now let us look at this masterpiece by Guido Reni carefully that we may know how wonderful is
the coming of day.

Aurora, in a filmy white robe, is dropping flowers in the path of
Apollo (the sun) as he drives his dun-colored horses above the
sleeping Earth. The Horæ (the hours), a gliding, dancing group of
lovely beings, accompany the brilliant god. Each hour is clothed in
garments of a special tint of the great light of day, red, orange, yel

low, green, blue, purple, and violet. The golden-hued Apollo sits supreme in his chariot of the sun.

The fresco—fresco means painted on fresh plaster—is on the ceiling of the Rospigliosi Palace, Rome. The painting is as brilliant in color to-day as it was when painted three hundred and fifty years ago.

Aurora, like most of the gods and goddesses, fell in love with a mortal. She asked Zeus to make her husband immortal but she forgot to ask that he should never grow old. And, fickle woman that she was! when he became gray and infirm, she deserted him and, to put a stop to his groans, she turned him into a grasshopper.

Her son, Memnon, was made king of the Ethiopians, and in the war of Troy he was overcome by Achilles. When Aurora, who was watching him from the sky, saw him fall she sent his brothers, the Winds, to take his body to the banks of a river in Asia Minor. In the evening the mother and the Hours and the Pleiades came to weep over her dead son. Poor Aurora! even to-day her tears are seen in the dewdrops on the grass at early dawn. [11]

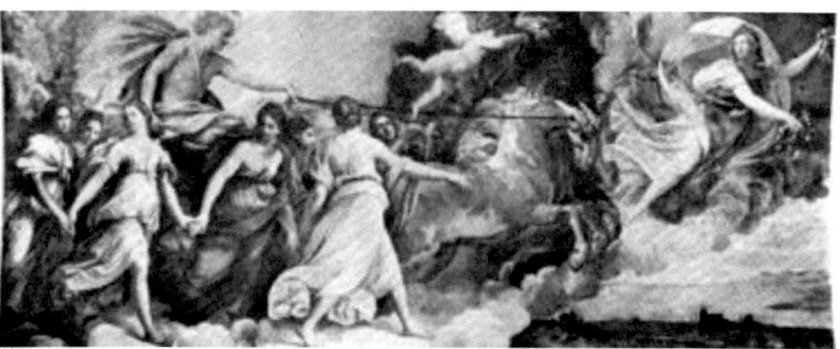

Courtesy of Pratt Institute

Fig. 5. The Aurora. Guido Reni. Rospigliosi Palace, Rome

[12]

THE SINGING BOYS

Frans Hals (1584?-1666)

T

hese jolly singers are Dutch boys. They are singing on the street or in some back yard just as singers do to-day, though they lived nearly three hundred years ago.

Hals was such a rapid painter that he could make a picture while you wait. The story is told that one time young Van Dyck, the Flemish painter who painted "Baby Stuart," went to see Hals in Amsterdam when Hals was an old man. Van Dyck did not tell the old artist that he was Van Dyck but simply asked him to paint his portrait, knowing what a rapid painter Hals was. In an hour the picture was done. Van Dyck remarked, as he looked at the portrait:

"That seems easy; I believe I could do it."

Hals thought he would have some fun, so he told the young stranger that he would sit for him just one hour.

Van Dyck set his easel where Hals could not see him work and began to paint. At the end of an hour he said:

"Your picture is finished, sir."

Hals, ready to laugh at the daub, looked at the portrait and the laugh went out of his face. He then looked at Van Dyck, and cried out:

"You must be either Van Dyck or a wizard!"

You see, Hals had heard of Van Dyck and his rapid work, and knew that only a master painter could make the splendid portrait in an hour. [13]

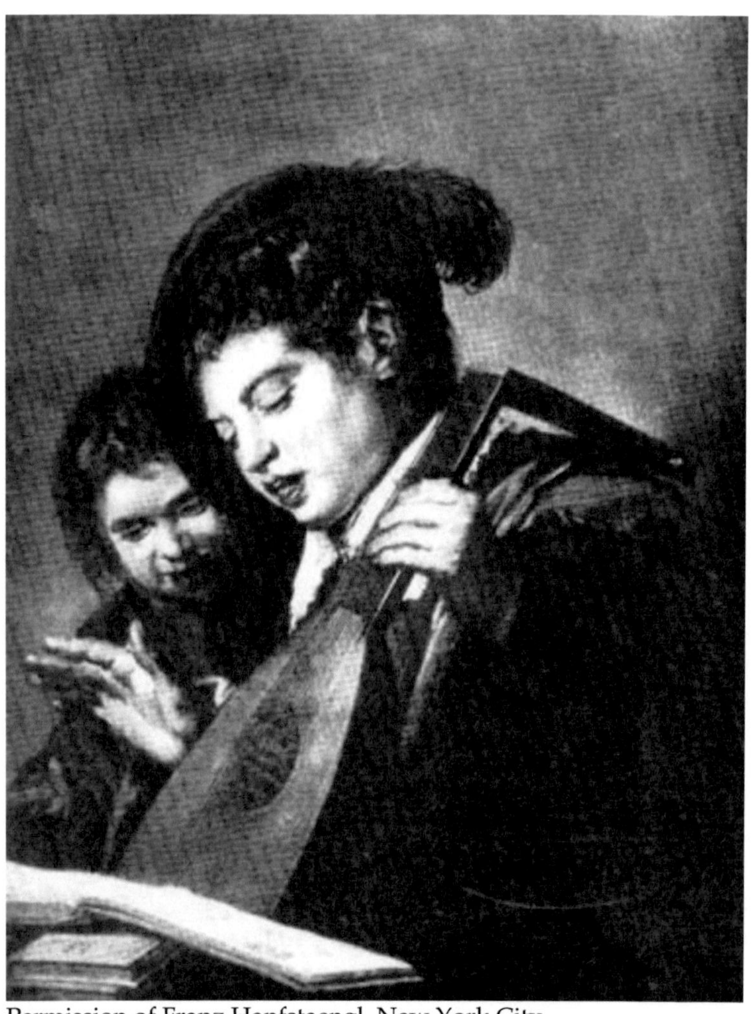

Permission of Franz Hanfstaengl, New York City

Fig. 6. Singing Boys. Frans Hals. Cassel Gallery, Germany
  [14]

18

ST. BARBARA

Jacopo Palma Il Vecchio (1480?-1528)

St. Barbara, born a. d. 303, was a very beautiful girl. Her father, an eastern nobleman, loved her so much and was so afraid something might happen to her that he built a very wonderful tower for her home and shut her up in it. And in that tower she studied the stars. Night after night she looked at the heavenly bodies until she knew more about the sun and the moon and the stars than any of the learned men. But as she studied the shining bodies she decided that worshiping idols, made of wood and stone, as her father did, was wrong. Finally she learned about the Savior, and to show her faith in Christianity she had some workmen who were making repairs on her tower put in three windows. When her father came as usual to visit her, he asked in surprise what the three windows were for. She replied:

"Know, my father, that through three windows doth the soul receive light, the Father, the Son, and the Holy Ghost: and the three are one."

Her father was very angry when he found she had learned about the Savior and had become a Christian. He condemned her to death and at last took her out on a hill and killed her, but he, too, was struck dead. St. Barbara is always represented with a tower that has three windows in it.

Palma Vecchio painted this picture for some Venetian soldiers nearly four hundred years ago. When the Germans bombarded Venice (1918) the Venetians took the picture from the church to a place of safety. Scarcely a week had passed before a bomb broke through the roof of the church tearing everything before it at the exact spot where the picture had hung. But "St. Barbara," one of the great pictures of the world, was safe. [15]

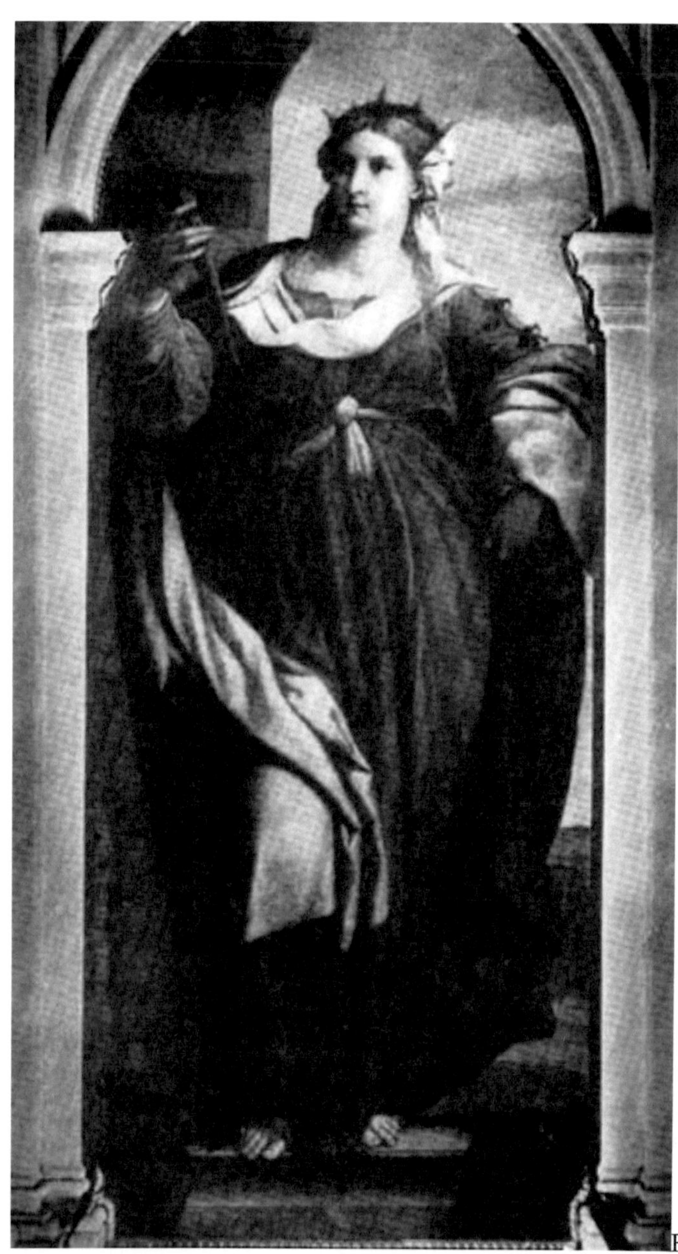

Fig. 7.

St. Barbara. Palma Vecchio. Santa Maria Formosa, Venice

[16]

CHARLES I AND HIS HORSE

Sir Anthony Van Dyck (1599-1641)

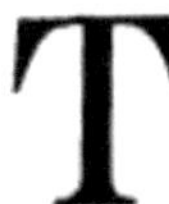

The horse in this picture of Charles I is probably the one Rubens gave to Van Dyck. It is said that Rubens gave it as a present after Van Dyck had painted a portrait of Helena Fourment, the master's second wife, and presented it to him. Van Dyck was twenty-two years younger than Rubens. You will remember that he was the master painter's favorite pupil. Having Rubens as a teacher did not make the pupil a great painter. Van Dyck was never more than a prince; just an heir to the throne. Rubens was a king and sat on the throne.

The story is told that once Rubens was away from his private studio when the students bribed the servant to open the door for them. They stole into the master's studio to see "The Descent from the Cross," which he was then painting. By some mishap the culprits rubbed against the wet paint and spoiled that part of the picture. Of course they were terrified at the damage done. They finally decided that Van Dyck was the one to repair the spot. The work was so well done that they hoped Rubens would not see the repairs. But the first thing that caught the eye of the master was that particular spot. He at once sent for the students and asked who had worked on his picture. Van Dyck stepped out from the others and frankly confessed that he was the culprit. Rubens was so pleased with his frankness and also at the skill of the work that he forgave them all.

King Charles I invited Van Dyck to come to England, and then he knighted him and gave him a pension for life. The hundreds of pictures of the royal family and court people of England left by Van Dyck show us how rapidly he could paint, for the artist died when he was only forty-two years old. [17]

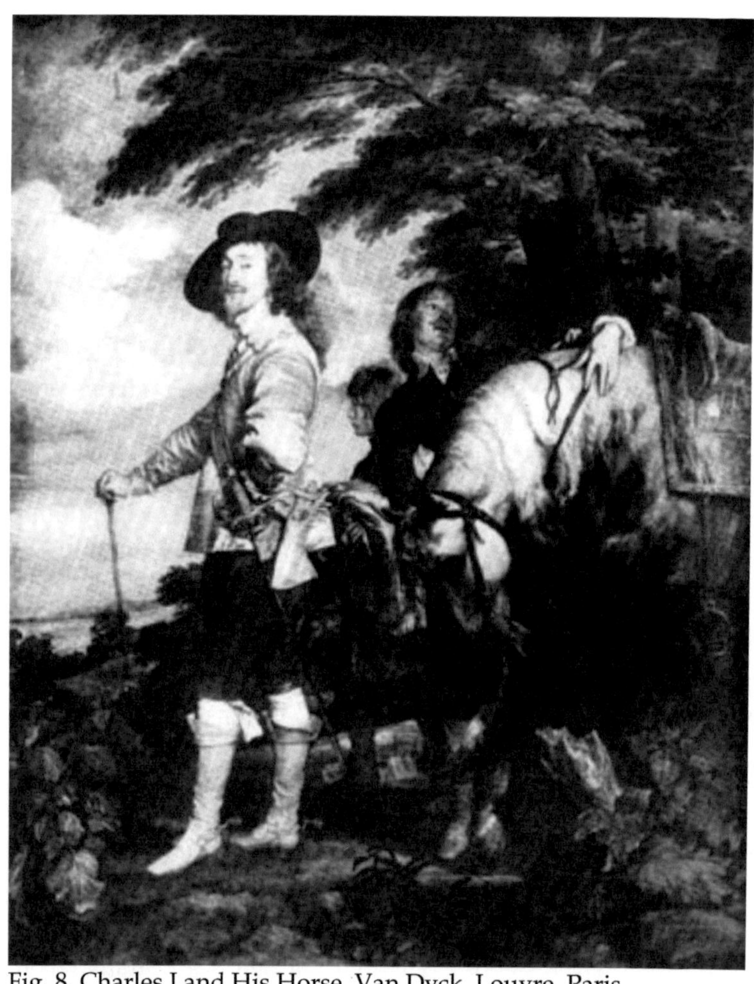

Fig. 8. Charles I and His Horse. Van Dyck. Louvre, Paris

   [18]

THE GALE

Winslow Homer (1836-1910)

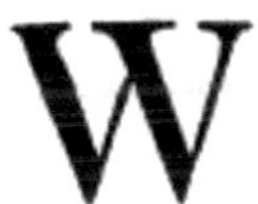

inslow Homer lived in Maine, where he heard the roar of mighty waters beating the rocks all day and all night. Some days the ocean grew so angry because the winds whirled its waters about in such a cruel manner that it would fling itself upon the sands and rocks as though to tear everything to pieces. The waves would raise up like furious horses champing their bits and foaming at the mouth. Somehow these angry waves could never go beyond a certain point, and the mother carrying her baby along the coast knows just the point at which the waves must stop. Let us clap our hands and shout with joy that old ocean cannot hurt that mother and her baby. Fill your lungs full of that glorious breeze whipping their hair and clothes. Open your eyes wide like the baby and let the salt air polish them until they sparkle like diamonds as the baby's do.

Winslow Homer loved old ocean, and so do we! Let us love his pictures of old ocean for he has taught us that that mighty power is under a greater Power. [19]

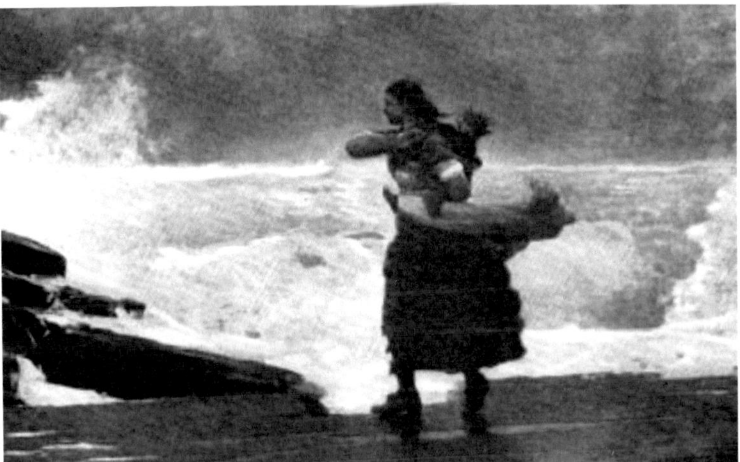

Fig. 9. The Gale. Homer. Courtesy of Worcester Art Museum, Massachusetts

[20]

MADONNA DEL GRAN' DUCA

Raphael Sanzio (1483-1520)

I want you to learn everything you can about Raphael. He was so kind and gentle and beautiful that everybody loved him. People said that when he walked on the streets of Rome scores of young men went with him until one would think him a prince. The pope gave him a large order to decorate the Vatican, the pope's home. Every artist was willing to help him because he was always ready to do anything he could to help his brother artists.

Raphael only lived to be thirty-seven. When he died all Italy mourned his death, and his funeral was one of the largest of any artist of his time.

When Raphael was only twenty-one he painted the "Madonna del Gran' Duca." He had gone to Florence for the first time. We do not know where the picture was for a hundred years after it was painted; then the painter Carlo Dolci owned it. Again another hundred years went by, and we find it in possession of a poor widow. She sold it to a picture-dealer for about twenty dollars. It then went into the hands of the grand duke of Tuscany, Ferdinand III, for the big sum of eight hundred dollars. No amount of money could buy the picture to-day.

Ferdinand loved the picture so much that he always took it with him on all his travels and the grand duchess, his wife, felt that her baby boys were purer if she had the picture near her. It got its name "Madonna of the Grand Duke" from the title of the family. [21]

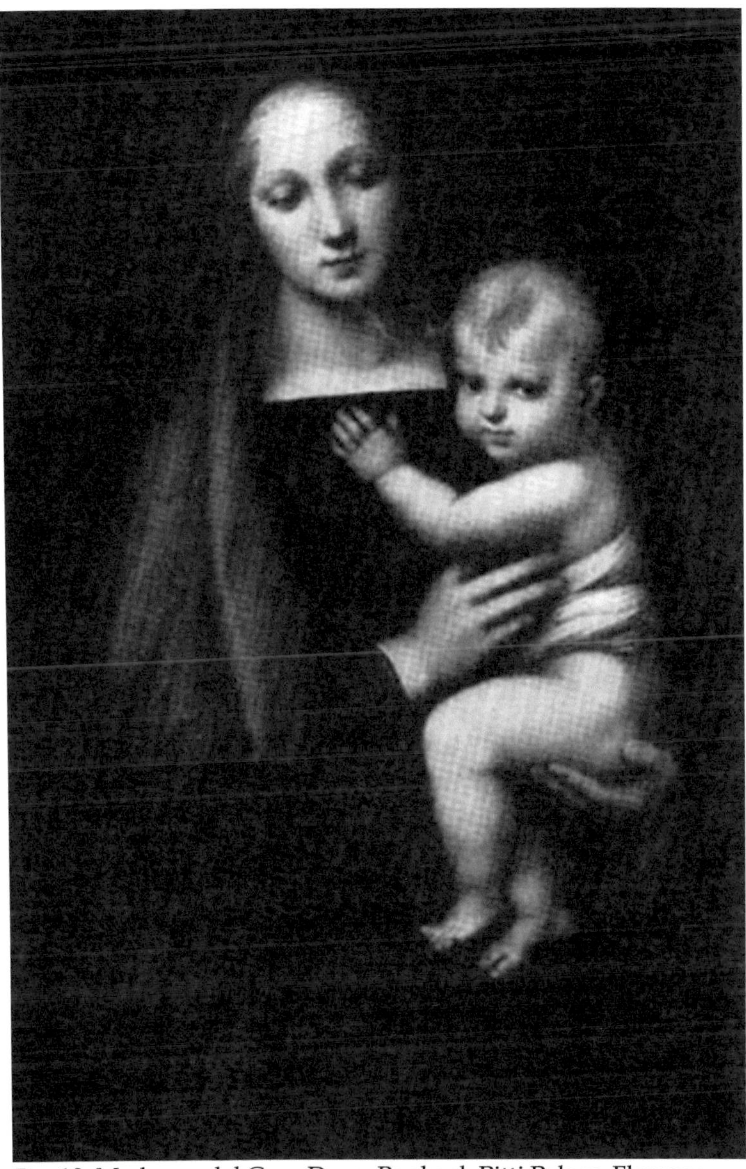

Fig. 10. Madonna del Gran Duca. Raphael. Pitti Palace, Florence

[22]

JOAN OF ARC

Jules Bastien-Lepage (1848-1884)

No young girl in history has had such a wonderful story as Joan of Arc. She began to hear voices and see visions when she was a little child. She was born in the tiny village of Domremy, France. Just like the other little peasant girls around her she helped her mother about the house and at the spinning. Also she went into the fields with her brothers.

One day when she was in the garden the Archangel St. Michael came to her in a glory of light. He said she was a good little girl and that she must go to church and that some day she was to do a great act; she was to crown the dauphin as king of France at Rheims. Joan was afraid and cried at what the angel told her, but St. Michael said, "God will help you."

These messages kept coming to her until, when she was sixteen, the voices insisted, "You must help the king, and save France."

France was in a terrible state at this time, 1428. The English held most of France. The French king, Charles VI, became insane and died. The son, Dauphin Charles, was weak and lazy and discouraged; he had no money, no army, no energy, and like most cowards, ran from his duty and wasted his time in wickedness.

Joan was still urged by voices to save France. At last a peasant uncle went with her to a man in power to ask for troops. The man was angry, and said sharply:

"The girl is crazy! Box her ears and take her back to her father." But Joan did not give up. She insisted that some one must take her to Dauphin Charles, that God willed it. She said:

"I will go if I have to wear my legs down to my knees." She went, and she saved France by crowning the dauphin as Charles VII at Rheims. But the French and the English people condemned Joan of Arc as a witch and burned her at the stake. Too late they cried:

"We are lost! We have burned a saint!" [23]

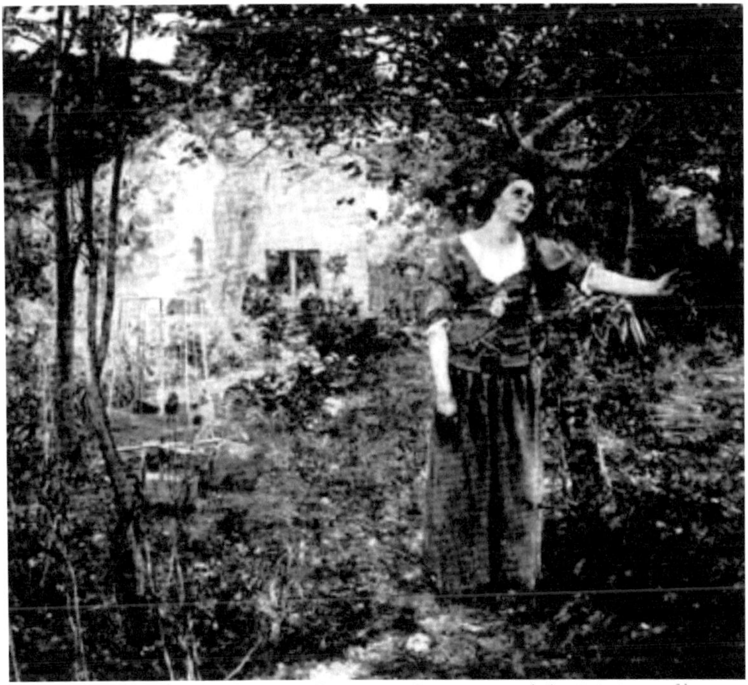

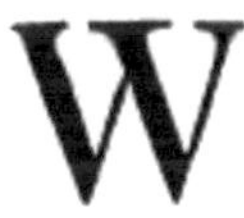

Fig. 11. Joan of Arc. Bastien-Lepage. Courtesy of the Metropolitan Museum of Art, New York City

[24]

THE FATES

Michael Angelo Buonarroti (1474-1564)

W

hen a new baby comes to a home, legend says, three beautiful young girls come to take care of the baby all through its life, but no one ever sees these young girls. Each one has a strange work to do. One, called Clotho, carries a spindle on which is wound flax. The second, named Lachesis, twists a thread from the spindle, called the thread of life. And Atropos, the third, has a pair of shears ready to cut the thread of life.

A funny story is told about Michael Angelo when he designed this picture of "The Fates." An old woman annoyed the artist very much by coming every day to see him. She insisted that he should appoint her son a special place in the fighting line in the seige of Florence (1529). Michael Angelo took revenge on the old woman by using her as a model for all of the women in his "Fates." And that is why Michael Angelo's fates are old women instead of young girls, as legend says they are. [25]

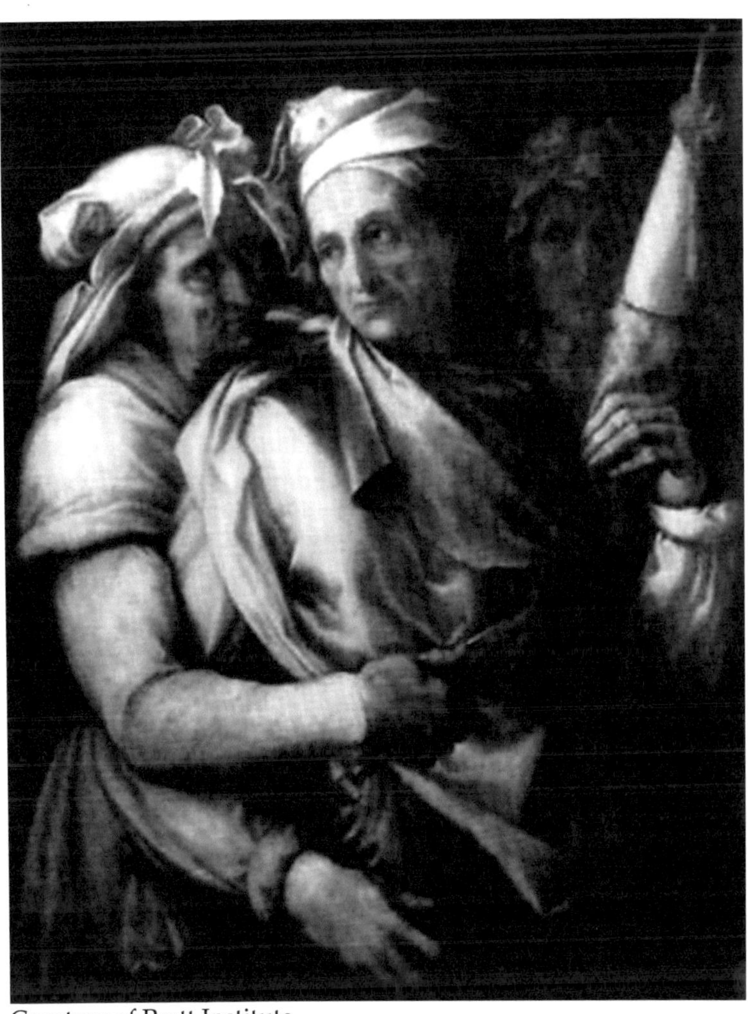

Courtesy of Pratt Institute

Fig. 12. The Fates. Michael Angelo. Pitti Palace, Florence
[26]

THE MADONNA OF THE CHAIR

Raphael Sanzio (1483-1520)

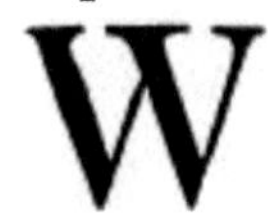

e like to believe that Raphael, in one of his daily walks in the country, really did see this mother and her two little boys sitting in a doorway. Of course he must paint them, and having no paper with him he rolled up a barrel and made a sketch on the head of it. The story says that this barrel was once a part of a great oak-tree that stood by the hut of an old man, a hermit up in the mountains. And the mother of the two boys, when a little girl, used to go to see the old man. He loved these two — the little girl and the big oak-tree — and called them his daughters.

He used to say that some day they would both be famous. That was more than four hundred years ago, and to-day this picture of "The Madonna of the Chair" is one of the most famous Madonna pictures. It is found in almost every home in America and is a treasure that belongs to all of us though it hangs in a gallery at Florence, Italy.

We know, too, that Raphael did not let any of his helpers work on "The Madonna of the Chair" — in Italian, "Madonna della Sedia." He painted every brush stroke himself, which makes it still more dear to us. [27]

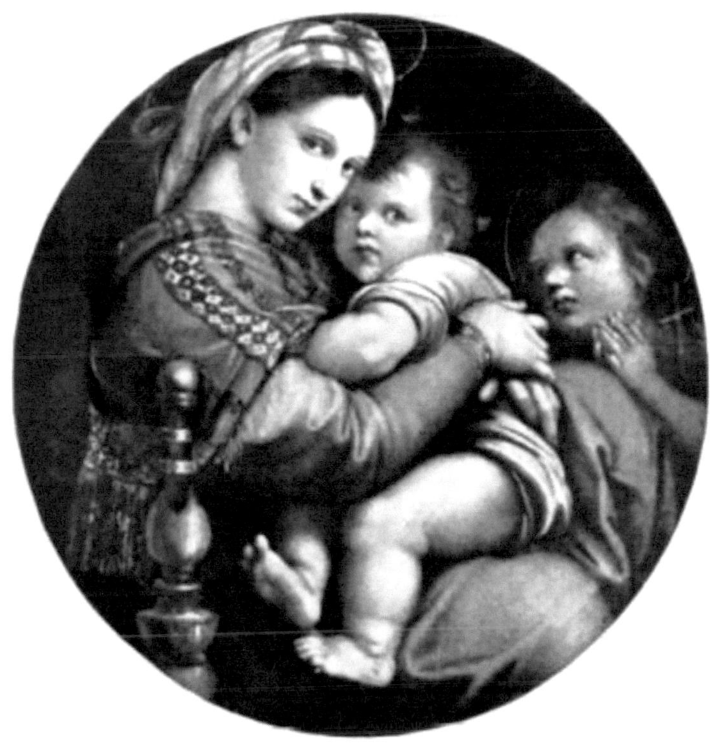

Courtesy of Pratt Institute

Fig. 13. Madonna of the Chair. Raphael. Pitti Palace, Florence

THE WOLF AND FOX HUNT

Peter Paul Rubens (1577-1640)

T he stables of Peter Paul Rubens were known the country over. No prince in the land had more magnificent horses, and no cavalier could ride with more grace and ease than Rubens.

When Van Dyck, the artist who painted "Baby Stuart," was ready to leave the studio of Rubens to travel in Italy, the master gave him a beautiful horse from his own stables. Van Dyck probably used this horse as a model in his picture of "Charles I and his Horse."

Now look at Rubens on the splendid dappled white horse in "The Fox and Wolf Hunt." His first wife, Isabel Brant, is on his right hand. She carries her falcon balanced on her wrist, his wings spread out in excitement. We feel that Rubens and his horse together are directing every movement in the hunt. That horse has all the alertness of the trained dogs and is just as eager in overcoming brute force as men are. In fact we are so fascinated with his beauty and intelligence that the cruel sport is almost forgotten in our interest in him and his master.

Rubens painted a number of hunting scenes, and always he manages the hunt with the skill of a master. The confusion of the rough-and-tumble fight between the wild beasts and the horses, dogs, and men in Rubens' pictures seems to untangle itself under his glorious color and skilful arrangement. This is a picture you must see. When you go to New York City never fail to visit the Metropolitan Museum of Art. [29]

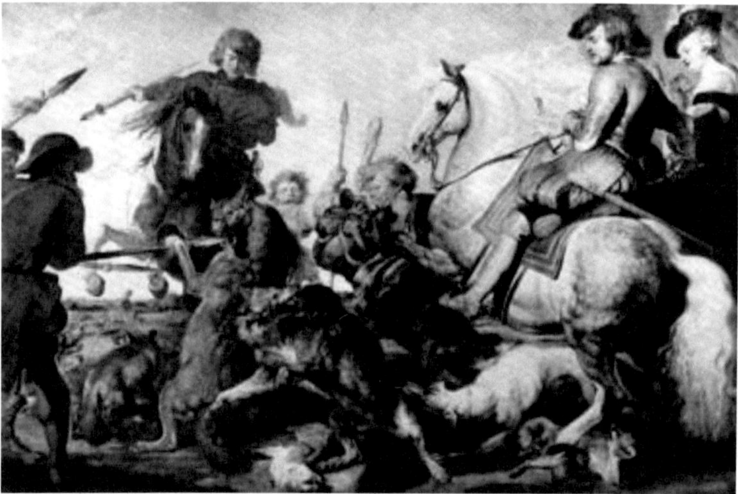

Fig. 14. Wolf and Fox Hunt. Rubens. Courtesy of the Metropolitan Museum of Art, New York City

THE NIGHT WATCH

Rembrandt Van Rijn (1607?-1669)

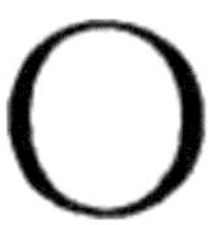

O ne time, more than two hundred and fifty years ago, two little children living in Amsterdam were playing at the edge of the city just at evening. Soon they overheard some Spanish soldiers near-by talking together. They began to understand that the men were making some kind of plans and, listening very sharply, they found that the Spaniards intended to attack the city of Amsterdam that night. The Spaniards were fighting the Netherlands at that time. You can imagine how frightened the children were. They knew that they must tell some one about it at once. Very quietly they crept away from where the men were, then ran for their lives to the town hall. The Civic Guard were having a banquet there. Rembrandt has painted the scene just as the little girl, in the center of the group, has finished her story. The men are making ready to meet the attack. Some have on their armor, some are polishing their guns, some have their drums, and all are full of excitement.

When the painting was to be put in the new Ryks Museum, in Amsterdam, it was found that the wall was too narrow for the picture. What do you think the authorities did? The stupid men cut a piece off from each side of the picture to fit it in its new place. Was ever anything so silly? Even those pieces cut off would bring more money to-day than the museum itself cost.

The men who had money at the time Rembrandt painted the picture were angry because the artist would not make portraits as they wanted them. They ignored Rembrandt, and he became very poor and died unknown. To-day those rich men are forgotten and Rembrandt is known the world over. [31]

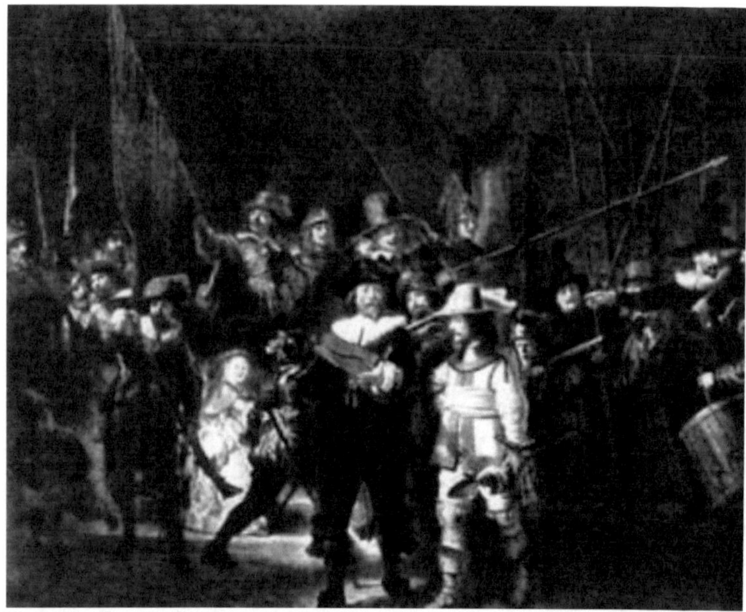

Fig. 15. The Night Watch. Rembrandt. Ryks Museum, Amsterdam

THE ASSUMPTION

Titian, or Tiziano Vecelli (1477-1576)

itian lived to be ninety-nine-years old and still painted pictures. He was working on a painting when an awful plague broke out in Venice, and he took it and died. Titian painted such wonderful pictures that kings came to see them and rich noblemen paid big sums of money to own them. Sometimes King Charles V would ride with Titian and would have his courtiers pay tribute to Titian and wait on him. This made those haughty men very jealous and very angry, but Charles V would say, "I have many nobles, but I have only one Titian."

Titian's picture of the "Virgin going to Heaven" the whole world calls one of the greatest pictures ever painted. Some day I hope you will go to Venice, that Queen City of the Sea, and fasten your gondola at the Museum door while you go in to see this picture. You will be so dazzled with its bright color that you will hardly see the little cherubs circling around the blessed mother. But I want you to look at them; they are darlings: then look at the men all reaching up and the Father in the sky looking down. The story of the picture is about Mary, the mother of Jesus, going to heaven. [33]

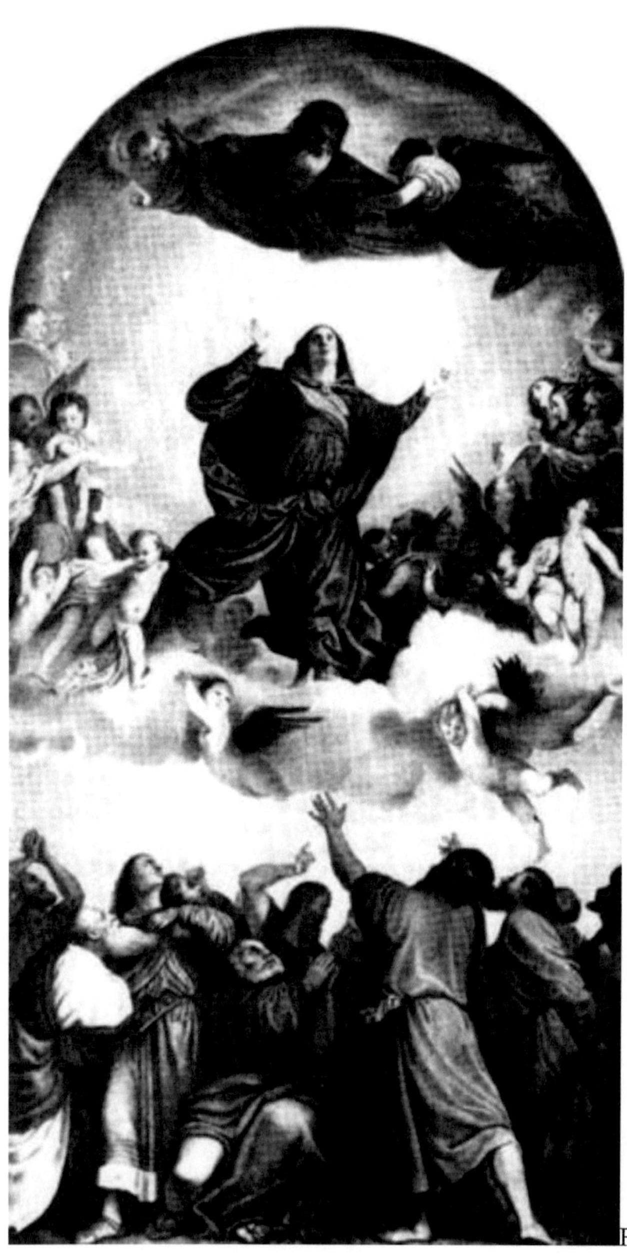

Fig. 16. The

Assumption. Titian. Academy, Venice

[34]

THE MELON EATERS

Bartolome Esteban Murillo (1618-1682)

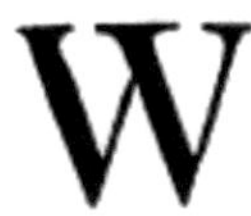

hen the Spanish artist Murillo was a young painter he was very poor and hardly knew where to get enough to eat. He would go to the market-place and set up his easel and rapidly paint the scenes around him. The people who came to the market to buy and sell saw these pictures and bought them for a mere pittance.

Often beggar boys, who were everywhere in the market snatching fruits and other eatables from the stalls, would pose for him as they hid in some corner to eat their stolen dainties. These beggar-boy pictures that Murillo sold for a song to keep his soul and body together began to attract attention until finally they were looked upon as the greatest pictures Murillo ever painted. People outside of Spain, Murillo's native country, bought them until to-day scarcely a beggar-boy picture of his is found in Spain.

This picture of "The Melon Eaters" is known far and wide as a great masterpiece, and yet the boys were little rag-a-muffins, the pests of the market people. Murillo knew the joys and sorrows of those boys because he too at that time was very poor and hungry and no one was giving him a helping hand. Do you suppose that when he was famous as a painter he ever saw those boys? I think so, for he was greatly beloved by his townspeople of Seville. They probably came to his studio many times. Murillo painted many religious pictures for the churches of Seville. [35]

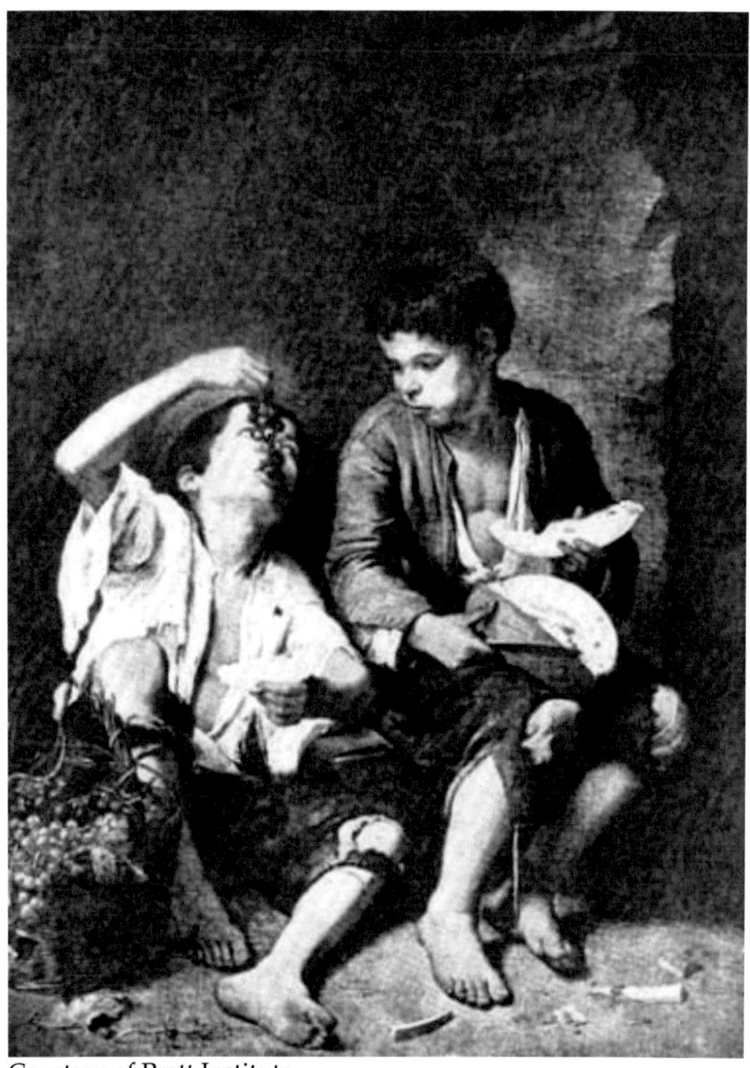

Courtesy of Pratt Institute

Fig. 17. The Melon Eaters. Murillo. Pinakothek, Munich
[36]

THE MUSES

Giulio Romano (1492-1546)

I am sure you have heard of the Muses. Romano, a pupil of Raphael's, has left us this beautiful picture of them dancing with Apollo, their cousin. The Muses were the daughters of Zeus (Jove or Jupiter), and Memory. These lovely girls also come to every home to help care for the new baby.

The Greek names of the Muses are rather hard to pronounce, but you will want to call them by name. Then, too, each girl's name in Greek letters is just below where she dances. Now begin at the left of the circle. The first one, Calliope, stands for narrative poetry; No. 2, Clio, is history; No. 3, Erato, is love-poetry; No. 4, Melpomene, is tragedy; No. 5, Terpsichore, is dance and song. Now comes Apollo with his quiver full of arrows. He is the god of the hunt and twin brother to Diana, the goddess of hunt; also he is god of music and poetry. No. 6 is Polyhymnia, muse of hymn-music; No. 7, Euterpe, is song poetry; No. 8, Thalia, is comedy, and No. 9, Urania, muse of astronomy.

Athene gave the Muses the winged horse, Pegasus. But alack and alas! one of the poets became very poor and sold Pegasus to a farmer. He was fastened to the plow, but he could not plow through the hard earth. His spirit was broken and his body was weak. The angry farmer tried to make him work, but how could he when he had no courage? But just then a beautiful youth came and asked the farmer to let him try the horse. Of course the man was glad to have any one help get the plowing done. The young man petted the horse and slyly unfastened the harness as he patted him. He mounted upon his back and Pegasus rose in the air, and away they both went, Pegasus and Mercury. The farmer looked on with amazement. How could a good-for-nothing horse that could not plow do such a wonderful thing as fly? [37]

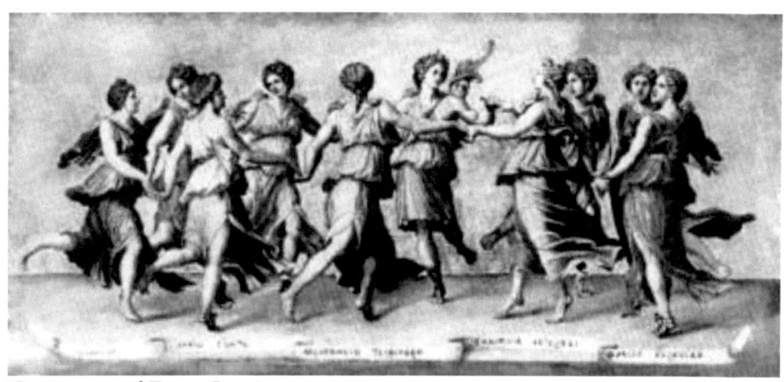

Courtesy of Pratt Institute

Fig. 18. The Muses. Romano. Pitti Palace, Florence

[38]

"COME, ABIDE WITH US"

Fra Giovanni Angelico (1387-1455)

Nearly two thousand years ago two men were walking together along a dusty road in Palestine. They talked earnestly as they walked along of a great event that had happened. A man called Jesus, the Christ, had been crucified and buried, but after three days he was not found in the tomb. As the men talked, a traveler joined them and asked:

"What is it ye talk about and are sad?"

And the men asked if he were a stranger in Jerusalem and did not know the things that had come to pass.

The stranger said, "What things?"

Then the men told him of Jesus of Nazareth, which was a prophet mighty in deed and word before God and all the people. And they said that they had all hoped He was the mighty one who was to save the world but that He had been killed.

Then the stranger, who was Jesus himself, but the men did not know Him, began to tell them the story of all things about himself. Still they did not know Him, and as they came to the village of Emmaus and the stranger made as though He would have gone further, the men said, "Come, abide with us."

This picture, showing the men inviting the stranger, was painted by Fra Angelico for the Dominican monastery in Florence, Italy. You will find it over the entrance of San Marco, where it welcomes every stranger who comes.

Fra Angelico was so kind and gentle and helpful that his companions called him "Angel Brother"; in Italian, "Fra Angelico." [39]

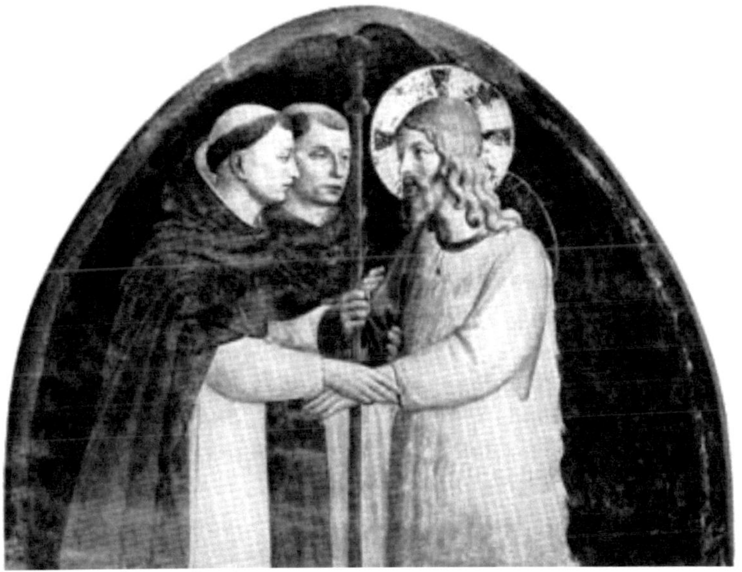

Courtesy of Pratt Institute

Fig. 19. "Come, Abide with Us." Fra Angelico. San Marco, Florence

[40]

THE SUPPER AT EMMAUS

Rembrandt Van Rijn (1607?-1669)

Rembrandt has taken the story of the two men and the stranger on their way to Emmaus after they have gone into the house. You see the disciples still did not know that the stranger was Jesus, the Christ. But when He sat at meat with them, He took bread and blessed it and brake and gave to them. Then they knew that it was the Savior who was talking with them and sitting at the table with them. Rembrandt shows the wondering men as they begin to recognize who their guest is, and he makes us feel the warmth and gladness that fill their hearts when they know that it is the risen Lord. The boy, too, lingers at the Savior's side as though to hear the meaning of the scene. But as they look, Jesus disappears out of their sight. When He is gone they say to each other:

"Did not our heart burn within us, while he talked with us by the way, and while He opened to us the Scriptures?"

Rembrandt painted this picture after many sorrows had come to him. His beloved Saskia, the mother of the "golden lad," Titus, was dead; friends had deserted him and his patrons were gone. But the love of people still filled the heart of the great painter. [41]

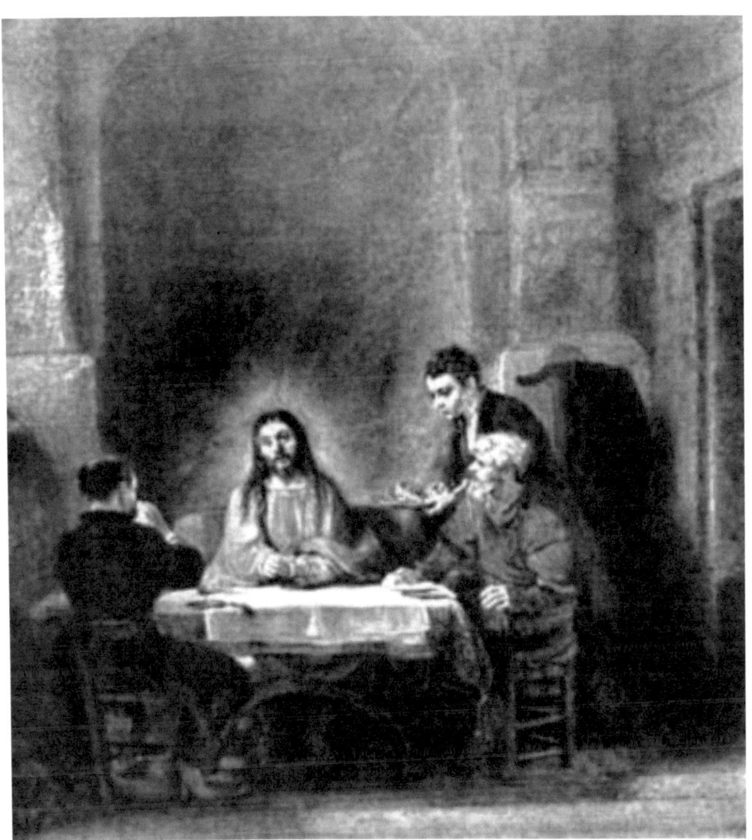

Fig. 20. The Supper at Emmaus. Rembrandt. Louvre, Paris

[42]

THREE CHILDREN OF CHARLES I OF ENGLAND

Sir Anthony Van Dyck (1599-1641)

T

he little boy standing between his brother and sister in this picture is Baby Stuart, the same child that is in the picture of "Baby Stuart" that you know so well. When Baby Stuart grew up he was crowned James II, king of England (1685). His brother was Charles II, king of England, and his sister was the mother of William III, king of England. James II, Baby Stuart, had a daughter, Mary, who became Mary, queen of England. When these cousins, William and Mary, grew up they were married and crowned king and queen of England in 1689.

A funny story is told of the crowning ceremony. William was very short and Mary was quite tall. It would not do to have Mary taller than her husband, so a stool was brought for William to stand on. Now they are the same height as they are crowned King William III and Queen Mary II of England. When William and Mary ruled England the country was happy and prosperous because love reigned in the royal household.

I have seen the stool that William stood on when he was crowned William III of England. It is in Westminster Abbey, London. That is another interesting bit of historic setting that you will see when you go to visit England.

Sir Anthony Van Dyck, the Flemish artist, painted many pictures of the royal families of England, especially the family of Charles I. He put little dogs into his pictures so often that the people began to call these little fellows "King Charles spaniels." To-day, two hundred years after, they are still called King Charles spaniels. [43]

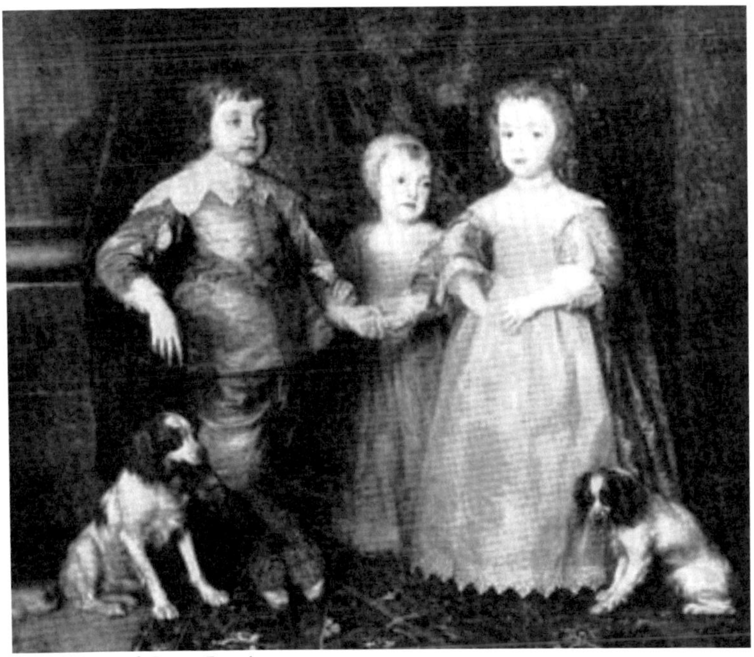

Courtesy of Pratt Institute

Fig. 21. Children of Charles I. Van Dyck. Dresden Gallery

[44]

THE BUTTERY

Pieter de Hooch (1632?-1681)

Pieter de Hooch is a Dutch artist you are going to love. Usually you can tell his pictures by the checked or plaid floors. The floors in the homes in Holland are mostly made of squares of black and white marble. Did you ever see a cuter little girl than this one in the picture? She has come for her pitcher of milk. Her mother went to the "buttery" for it: a buttery is a place for keeping casks and barrels and bottles. We can see one end of the cask or barrel under the window in the buttery. Now look into the next room and see the chair on a little platform. That platform is quite common in the Dutch home and is probably the place where mother or grandmother sits to read or sew by the window. What a beautiful day it must be out of doors to make the rooms so cheerful and bright! Hooch loved the sunshine and used it to brighten every home he painted. The sunshine on the checked floors makes his pictures sing with joy and happiness.

We can find very little about the life of the "Dutch little masters," yet the pictures they have left us are among our greatest treasures: just little home scenes that you and I know about.

It is said that de Hooch often put in his people after he had finished painting his picture. In one picture he has added a girl near a fireplace to make the picture more balanced. We know that she was added after the picture was made, for we can see the plaid floor through her dress where the paint was too thin to cover the original floor. Such little things tell us something of the method of work of the Dutch painters. [45]

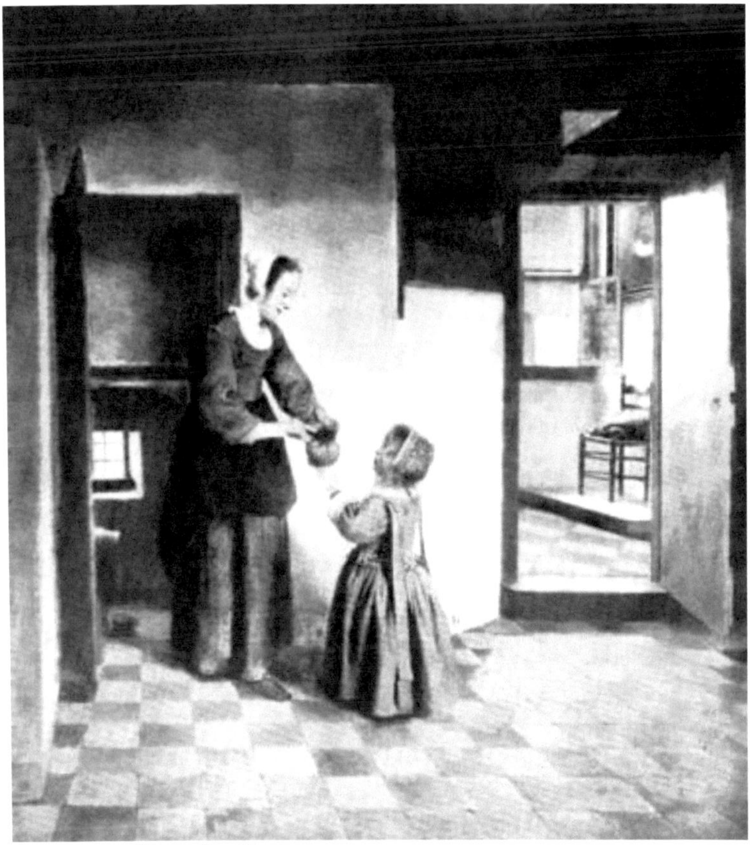

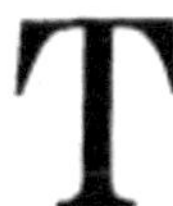

Courtesy of Pratt Institute

Fig. 22. The Buttery. De Hooch. Ryks Museum, Amsterdam
   [46]

THE CORONATION OF THE VIRGIN

Sandro Botticelli (1446-1510)

T

he children who are holding the book and ink-bottle in this picture, "The Coronation of the Virgin," lived four hundred years ago. Their names are Giovanni and Giulio de' Medici. Botticelli, the artist, knew them well for he was born and brought up in Florence and used to spend a great deal of time at the Medici Palace.

The boys were cousins. Giulio, the younger, was left an orphan when a wee child and his uncle, Lorenzo the Magnificent, adopted him and had him brought up with his own son Giovanni. The boys were nearly the same age and grew up to be great and good men. Both of them were popes of Rome. The older boy, Giovanni, was Pope Leo X and Giulio Pope Clement VII.

Now look at the picture again. The Madonna is reading to her little son, Jesus, "The Magnificat," that beautiful song from Luke, Chap. I, v. 46-56, sung so often in our churches. Let us repeat the song together:

> My soul doth magnify the Lord,
> And my spirit hath rejoiced in God my Savior.
> For He hath regarded the low estate of his handmaiden:
> For, behold, from henceforth, all generations shall call me blessed.
> For He that is mighty hath done to me great things; and holy is His name.
> And His mercy is on them that fear Him from generation to generation
> He hath shewed strength with his arm;
> He hath scattered the proud in the imagination of their hearts.
> He hath put down the mighty from their seats,
> And exalted them of low degree.
> He hath filled the hungry with good things;
> And the rich he hath sent empty away.
> He hath holpen his servant Israel, in remembrance of his mercy;
> As He spake to our fathers, to Abraham, and to his seed for ever.
> [47]

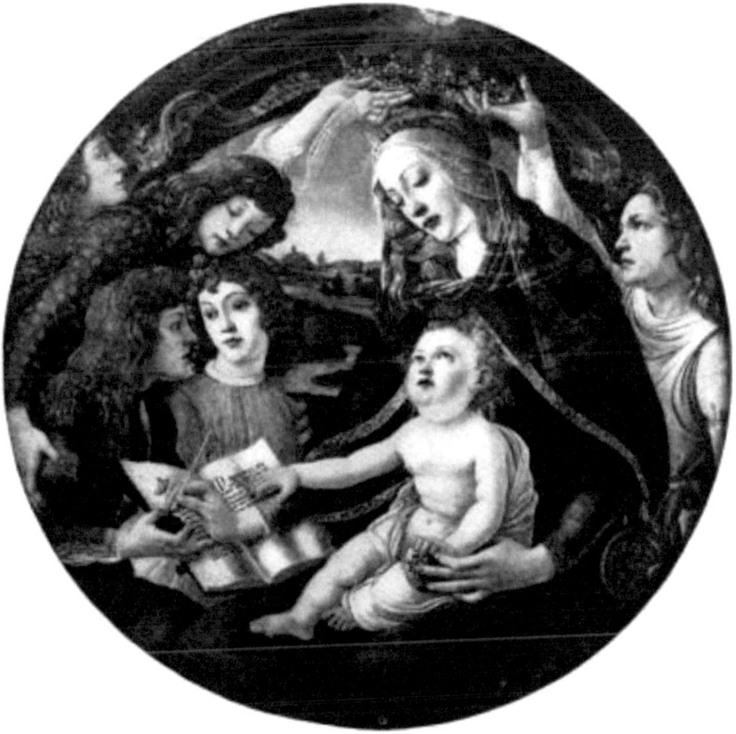

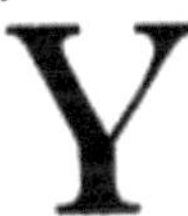

Fig. 23. Coronation of the Virgin. Botticelli. Uffizi Palace. Florence

[48]

THE WOLF CHARMER

John La Farge (1835-1910)

Y ou see these wolves were once the old women gossips of the town, the story says; and when these women were unkind in what they said about people the Fates—I have told you another story

about the Fates—the Fates to punish them turned them into wolves.
The Wolf Charmer, who really is the old gypsy who killed the black
cat of the village witch, goes out into the night. The owl calls the
wolves to attack the gypsy. But the gypsy knew the old women
before they were turned into wolves so he calls them by name:
"Kate, Anne, and Bee!" And soon they follow him down the narrow
path between the rocks and listen to his music on the bagpipes. "A
funny story!" you say. You know there are people who have a
strange power over wild animals.

John La Farge said about this picture, "I made it to be one of a series of some hundred subjects, more or less fantastic and imagi-
nary." He never finished the pictures nor carried out his plan of
making these books for children. I am giving you "The Wolf
Charmer" because he painted the picture for you. Mr. La Farge
named this picture as the one he liked best of his paintings. [49]

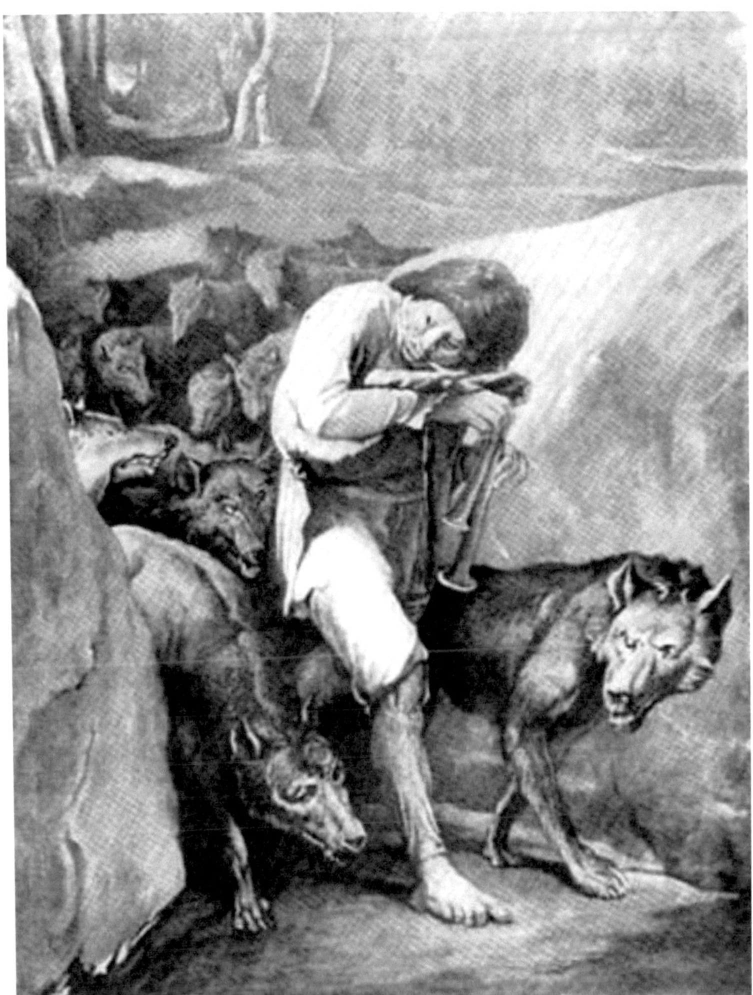

Courtesy of John La Farge

Fig. 24. The Wolf Charmer. La Farge. Courtesy of the City Art Museum, St. Louis

[50]

THE OLD WOMAN CUTTING HER NAILS

Rembrandt Van Rijn (1607?-1669)

No artist in all history had a sadder life than Rembrandt. It was sad because the people of Amsterdam were stupid and too blind to know that a great man was living among them. Rembrandt could paint wonderful portraits, and the rich people wanted their portraits painted. At first all went well. The rich flocked to his studio and Rembrandt made marvelous likenesses. Then the guilds of the great commercial houses wanted pictures for their halls. They came to Rembrandt for these pictures, but thinking that their money had bought the great artist body and soul, they began to tell him how he should make the pictures that each one might have equal prominence in it. Naturally Rembrandt would not be bought off with money. His art was bigger than gold. The picture that was really the turning point in his life was "The Night Watch." I wish you would look at the picture again. You see the men away back in the picture were jealous that they were not put in the front row. All they cared for was to have a fine portrait of themselves and Rembrandt was only interested in making a great picture.

Rembrandt went on painting but no one bought his pictures. Many sorrows came to him. It was when the world had forsaken him that he painted "The Old Woman Cutting her Nails." Now you can understand why Rembrandt could paint an old woman with human sympathy. We could love that old woman because the unkindness of the world made her more tender and true to suffering humanity. She is the old grandmother we would go to if we were in trouble. [51]

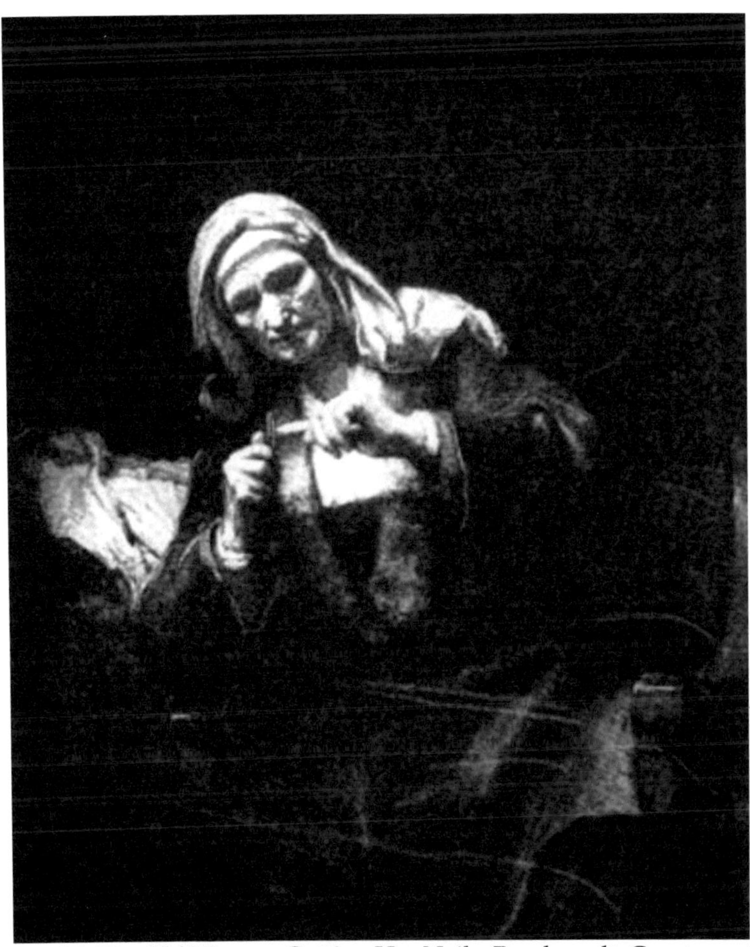

Fig. 25. The Old Woman Cutting Her Nails. Rembrandt. Courtesy of the Metropolitan Museum of Art, New York City

[52]

THE SPINNER

Nicolaes Maes (1632-1693)

his old woman is spinning flax. Have you ever seen a flax wheel? When you go to Holland try to visit Dordrecht, and if possible, go into a real Dutch home. There you may see some one, the grandmother maybe, spinning flax; then you will know that this picture is an actual scene.

Nicolaes Maes, who painted the picture, was born in Dordrecht or Dort. This city is said to be the oldest city in the Netherlands; it was founded in the tenth century. An old woman spinning was a familiar scene to Maes. Now look at this spinner closely. She will not mind, for she is too intent on picking up a thread, possibly a broken or a knotted one. Maes saw a picture in the old woman's dull red dress and bright red sleeves. He liked the brown wheel and the yellow floor and the beautiful bit of blue cloth thrown over the wheel-base. Then he saw how beautifully the white kerchief and apron and wall caught the light. He saw the helpfulness of the rugged old hand, worn and scarred as it was, yet patient and firm in repairing a mistake.

Maes's "The Spinner" and Rembrandt's "The Old Woman Cutting her Nails" make the tasks of every-day life very human. We in America owe much to these old Dutch women and to the artists who have made them live for us.

This picture of "The Spinner" is only sixteen and one fourth inches high and thirteen inches wide, yet that old woman at her spinning-wheel is as much a real person in the room where she hangs on the wall as she was when Maes painted her, nearly three hundred years ago. I want you to love these little Dutch pictures; they are so honest and true and tell us about real people and real things, and they make us feel that beauty is everywhere. Now look at your grandmother as she mends your stockings and see how beautiful she is with the light on her dear old face and hair. [53]

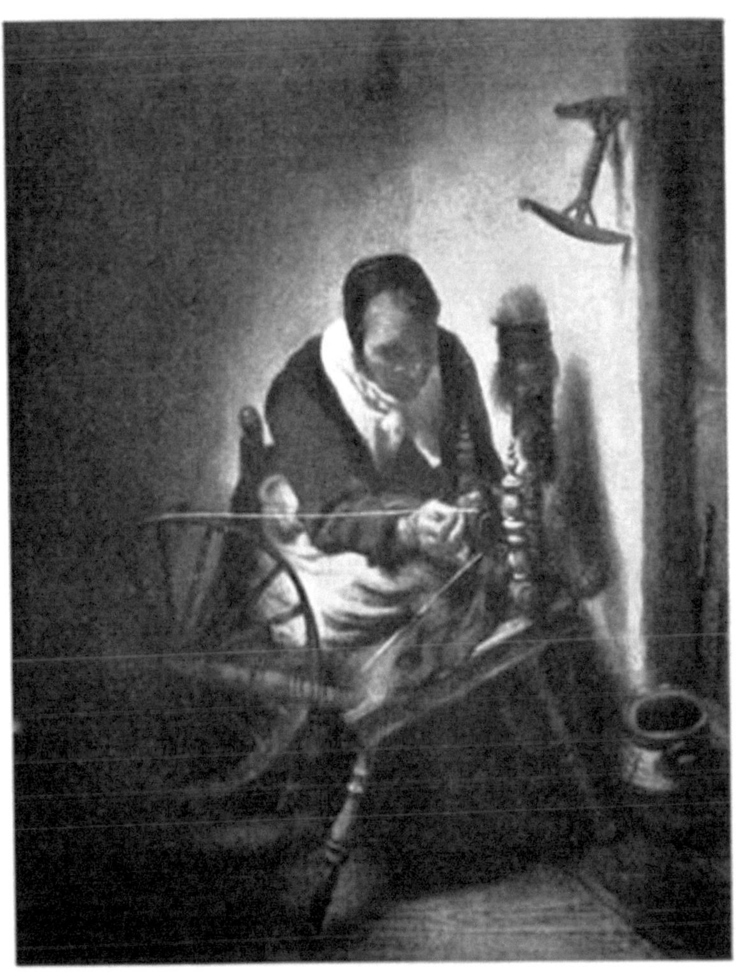

Fig. 26. The Spinner. Maes. Ryks Museum, Amsterdam
[54]

ST. GEORGE AND THE DRAGON

Vittore Carfaccio (1440?-1522)

S

t. George, a noble youth of Cappadocia, was one of the oldest and most noted of the saints. The story always told of him is his killing the dragon. Once upon a time St. George was going through Palestine on horseback when he came to the City of Beirut. There he found a beautiful young girl in royal dress weeping outside the walls of the city. When he asked her why she was crying, she told him that a terrible dragon lived in the marshes near the city. And to keep him from destroying every one in the city, each day two young girls must be fed to him. These young girls were chosen by lot, and this day she, Cleodolinda, the king's daughter, must be eaten by the dragon.

St. George told her not to be afraid for he would destroy the dragon. But she cried:

"O noble youth, tarry not here, lest thou perish with me! but fly, I beseech thee!" St. George answered:

"God forbid that I should fly! I will lift my hand against the loathly thing, and will deliver thee through the power of Jesus Christ!"

Then St. George, rushed at the dragon and thrust his spear into his mouth and conquered him. He then took the young girl's mantle and bound the beast, and she led him into the city to her father. That day twenty thousand people of the city were baptized.

As time went on the name of St. George became very great. From the time that Richard I—the Lion-Hearted—placed his army under the protection of St. George the saint became the patron saint of England. In 1330 the order of the Garter, the highest order of knighthood in Great Britain, was founded and on its emblem is a picture of St. George and the dragon.

Carpaccio, a Venetian artist, painted this picture of "St. George and the Dragon." He painted many other stories of saints. [55]

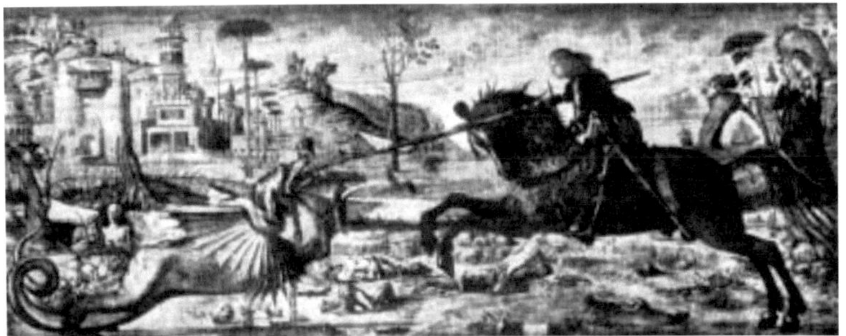

Fig. 27. St. George and the Dragon. Carpaccio. Church of San Giorgio degli Schiavoni, Venice

[56]

THE GRAND CANAL, VENICE

Joseph Mallard William Turner (1775-1851)

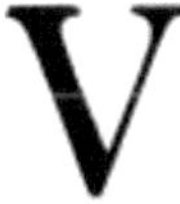

Venice is a very curious city. It is really built on stilts on top of the water. Its streets are canals. Instead of having street-cars and horses and taxicabs everybody goes in long boats called gondolas. The main street in the city is the Grand Canal, and in this canal come all sorts of people with all sorts of water-crafts.

The children play in the side streets just as you do except that they swim in the water instead of running on the ground. Even the babies are in the water fastened to the door-steps by a rope around their little bodies. How they do coo and gurgle as they paddle their little hands and feet like young frogs!

Turner shows in this picture the Grand Canal filled with ships from other countries with gaily colored flags fluttering in the breeze. Do you see the tower at the left in the picture? That is the Campanile, the bell-tower. This wonderful tower fell down flat in 1902. I talked with a man who has a store just opposite the tower, a few weeks after it fell. He said to me: "I thought it would fall on my store and destroy everything. It began to tip; then all at once it fell flat just where it stood." The Venetians soon built it up again.

When Napoleon, the great French emperor, took Venice, he rode up the inclined plane of this tower on his horse and stood on the very top overlooking the sea. [57]

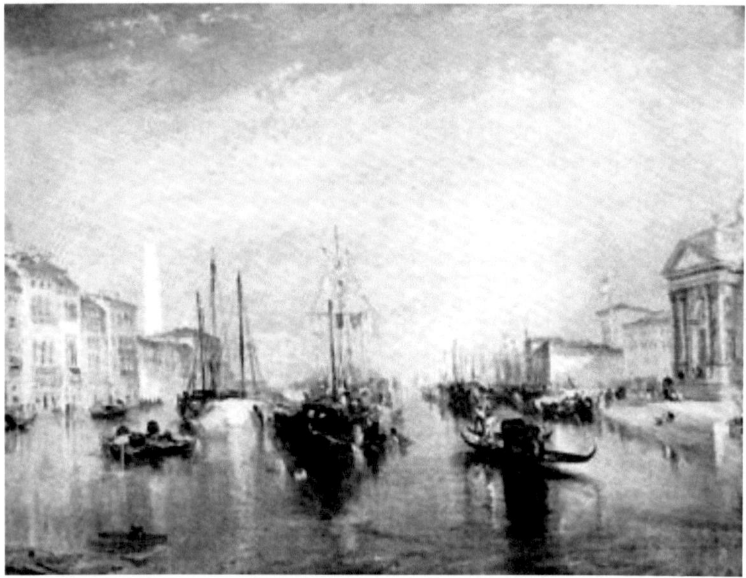

Fig. 28. The Grand Canal. Turner. Courtesy of the Metropolitan Museum of Art, New York City

[58]

THE SONG OF THE LARK

Jules Adolphe Breton (1827-1906)

> Up with me! up with me into the clouds!
> For thy song, Lark, is strong;
> Up with me, up with me into the clouds!
> Singing, singing,
> With clouds and sky above thee ringing,
> Lift me, guide me till I find

That spot which seems so to thy mind!

Wordsworth

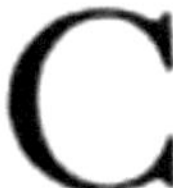

an you not almost hear this girl singing? The sun is just coming up. The lark is rising in the sky, singing! The girl has come out to work in the fields; a peasant girl. Barefooted, barehanded, she stands straight like a soldier of work with her head lifted to drink in the morning air as she sings.

One morning early I was driving through the country roads in the south of England when larks began to rise from the fields where the workmen were, just like this lark from the French field, and how they did sing! I stopped and listened, watching them go up higher and higher, their song growing fainter and fainter, and then they disappeared. Where did they go? Let us ask this French peasant girl. Do you think that she can tell us? If she cannot, who can? [59]

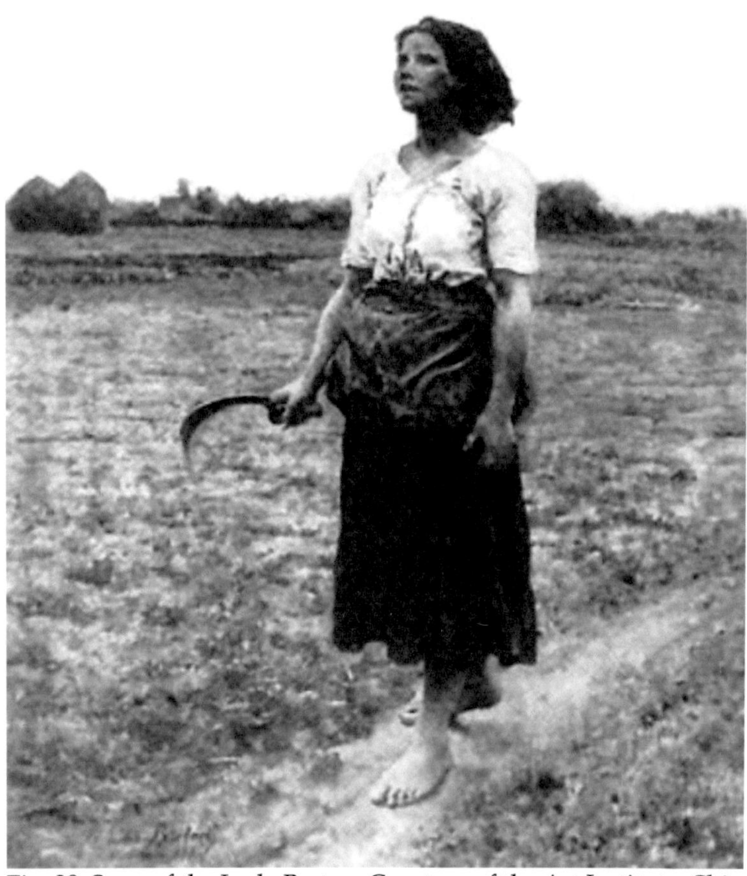

Fig. 29. Song of the Lark. Breton. Courtesy of the Art Institute, Chicago

[60]

THE HOLY NIGHT

Antonio Allegra da Correggio (1494?-1534)

I t is a wonderful story, the story of the Holy Night. The mother and father had traveled a long way; and when they came to Bethlehem every place was taken so they found a bed in a cave. In the night a baby boy came to the mother, and she "wrapped Him in swaddling clothes, and laid Him in a manger, because there was no room for them in an inn. And there was in the same country shepherds abiding in the fields, keeping watch over their flocks by night. And, lo, the angel of the Lord came upon them, and the glory of the Lord shone around about them; and they were sore afraid.

"And the angel said unto them, Fear not; for behold, I bring you good tidings of great joy, which shall be to all people. For unto you is born this day in the city of David, a Savior, which is Christ, the Lord. And this shall be a sign unto you; ye shall find the babe wrapped in swaddling clothes, lying in a manger. And suddenly there was with the angel a multitude of the heavenly host praising God, saying, Glory to God in the Highest, and on earth peace, good will unto men.

"And it came to pass as the angels were gone away from them into heaven, the shepherds said one to another, Let us go even to Bethlehem and see this thing which has come to pass, which the Lord has made known to us. And they came with great haste, and found Mary and Joseph; and the babe lying in a manger. At first a bright cloud overshadowed the cave but on a sudden the cloud became a great light in the cave, so that their eyes could not bear it. But the light gradually decreased until the Infant appeared, and sucked the breast of his mother, Mary."

The picture shows us the shepherds in the cave worshiping the young child, Jesus, the Christ. [61]

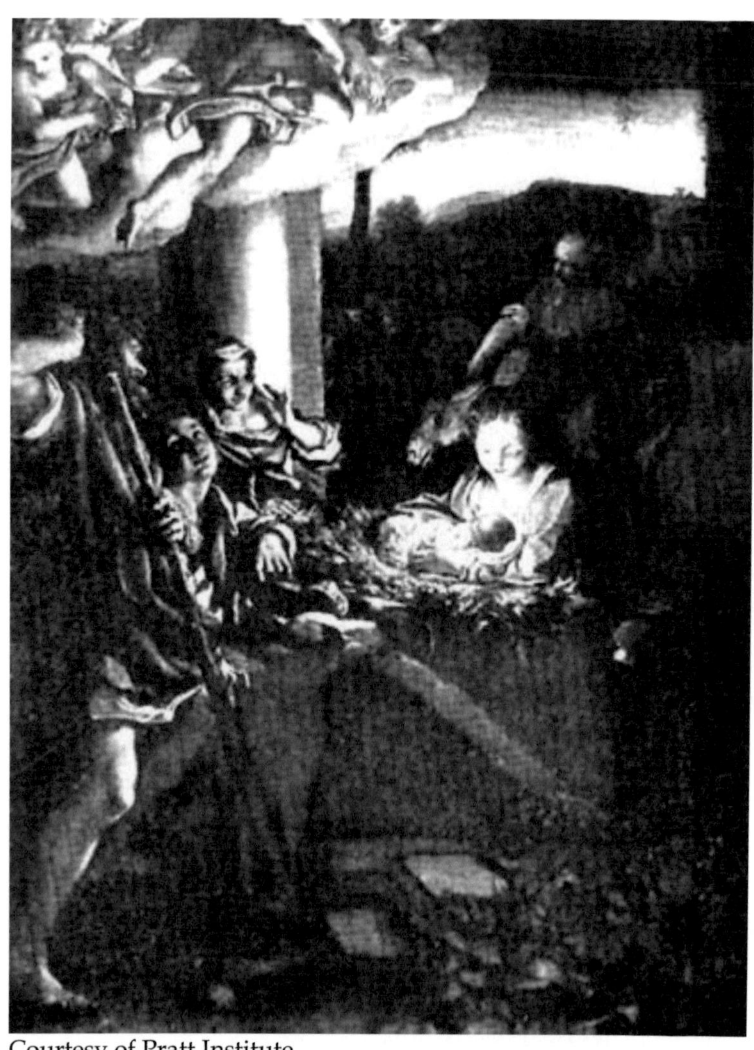

Courtesy of Pratt Institute

Fig. 30. The Holy Night. Correggio. Dresden Gallery
  [62]

THE GLEANERS

Jean François Millet (1814-1875)

Millet was a French peasant boy — very poor. He says his grandmother would come into his room early in the morning and call:

"Awake, my little François; if you only knew how long a time the birds have been singing the glory of the good God!"

He would insist when he was helping in the fields that there was beautiful color over the plowed ground, and when the other fellows laughed at him, he would say:

"Wait, some day I will paint a picture and show you the color."

After he was an artist he was going by a field one day when a peasant cutting grain called to him:

"I would like to see you take a sickle."

"I'll take your sickle," Millet answered quickly, "and reap faster than you and all your family."

Of course the man laughed, for how could an artist cut grain. He soon stopped laughing, for Millet cut much faster and farther than he could.

Millet would often go into the forest just back of his house to rest after painting all day. Then he would say:

"I do not know what those beggars of trees say to each other, but they say something which we do not understand, because we do not understand their language."

Millet's work is often called "the poems of the earth."

Once when I was in Barbizon I found the gate open into Millet's door-yard. Of course I walked in, but the owner insisted that I walk out again. I shall never forget the peep I had of the little garden and the doorway and the long rambling house. That Millet lived there with his large family and there painted the pictures we love makes the place a joy to us. [63]

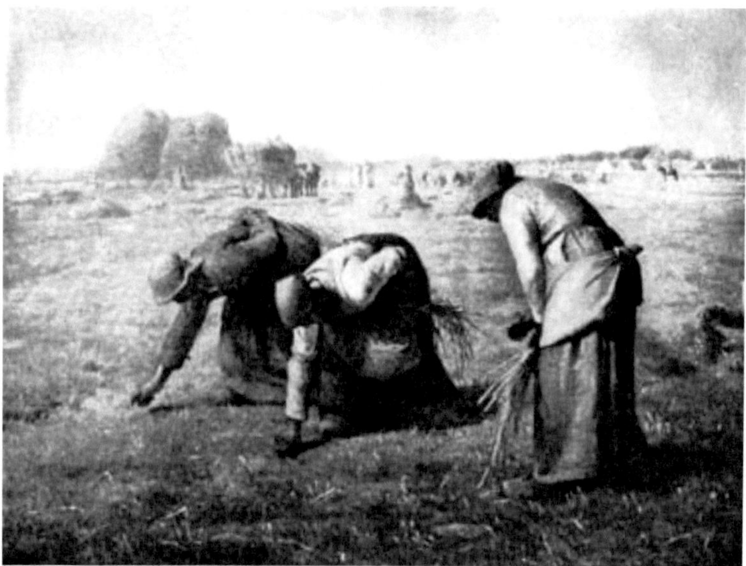

Fig. 31. The Gleaners. Millet. Louvre, Paris

ST. CECILIA

Raphael Sanzio (1483-1520)

Did you know that St. Cecilia invented the organ, that wonderful musical instrument in our churches? Cecilia was born in Rome sixteen hundred years ago. She was a beautiful young girl who loved music and composed many hymns. The organ she dedicated to God's service.

When Cecilia was married, her husband, a rich nobleman, was converted and baptized. He knelt by the side of Cecilia, and an angel crowned them with crowns made from roses which bloomed in paradise. The first thing Valerian asked was that his brother, who was a heathen, might be converted too. They sent for the brother, and when he came and found the room filled with the sweet fragrance of roses, though it was not the rose season, then he too became a Christian.

The people of Rome were very unkind to Cecilia and Valerian and his brother because they preached the story of Jesus, the Christ. At last they killed them. St. Cecilia is the guardian saint of music and is always shown in art with the organ, as you see in this picture by Raphael. The man standing at the left of the picture with his hand up to his face is St. Paul. This is the most famous picture of St. Paul. Raphael shows the group listening to the heavenly choir while the earthly instruments of music have fallen at Cecilia's feet broken and out of tune. [65]

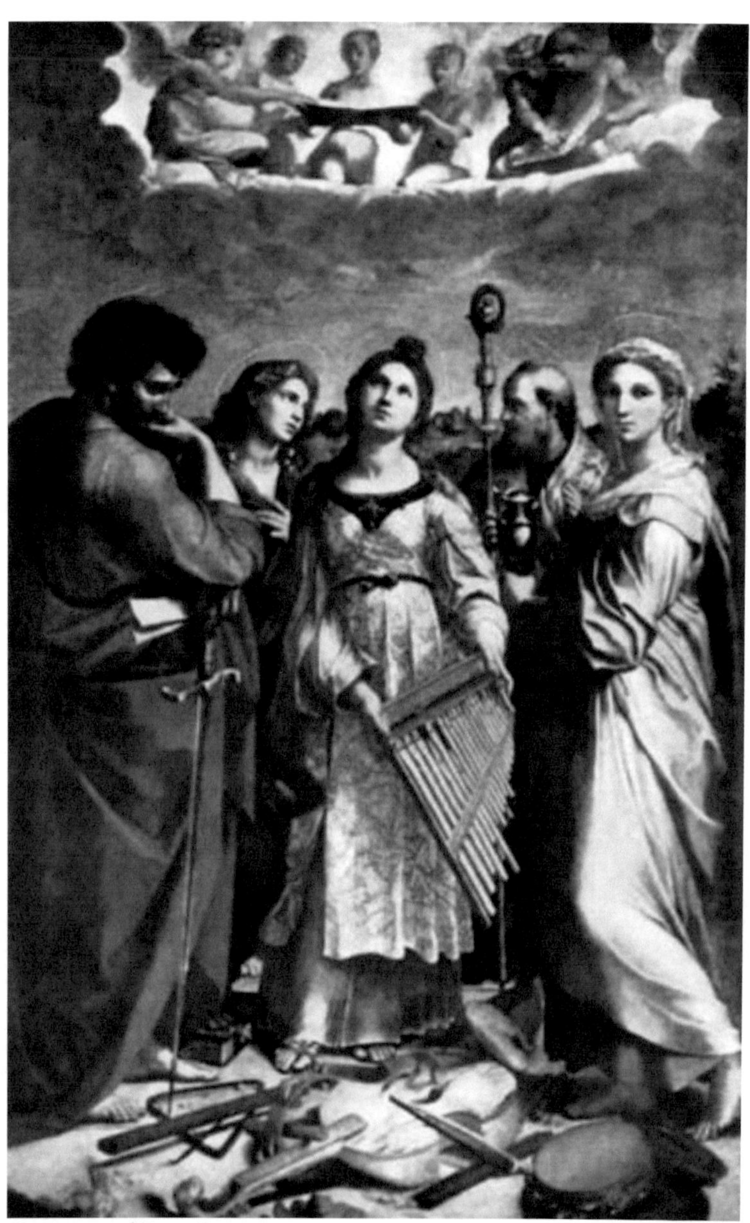

HELENA FOURMENT RUBENS AND HER SON AND DAUGHTER

Peter Paul Rubens (1577-1640)

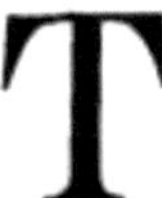his picture of "Helena Fourment Rubens and Her Son and Daughter" was really painted to honor the boy. It has always been the custom in Europe to pay special attention to the boys in the home and keep the girls very much in the background. It is very easy to see how pert the little Albert Rubens is, and how subdued and meek is his sister. The boy has the "Lord of Creation" air that would not be good for him in America. We love the picture, for Rubens, the father, shows us plainly the old idea that the boy rules the home. Naturally the father would know the traits of his own children but not always would he allow us to know them too.

Rubens was so wonderful as an artist, as a man to settle quarrels, and as a beautiful gentleman that all Europe did him honor. He was sent to see the ruling powers in England, in Spain, in Italy, and in France. Each ruler entertained him as a royal guest, and Rubens painted masterpieces for each in return. His paintings were the wonder of the age. It is said that his fellow-artists looked with jealous eyes at his flesh tints, and that all painters since have been in despair trying to equal him. He left hundreds of pictures and hundreds of sketches. The sketches alone are bringing many hundreds of times their weight in gold. [67]

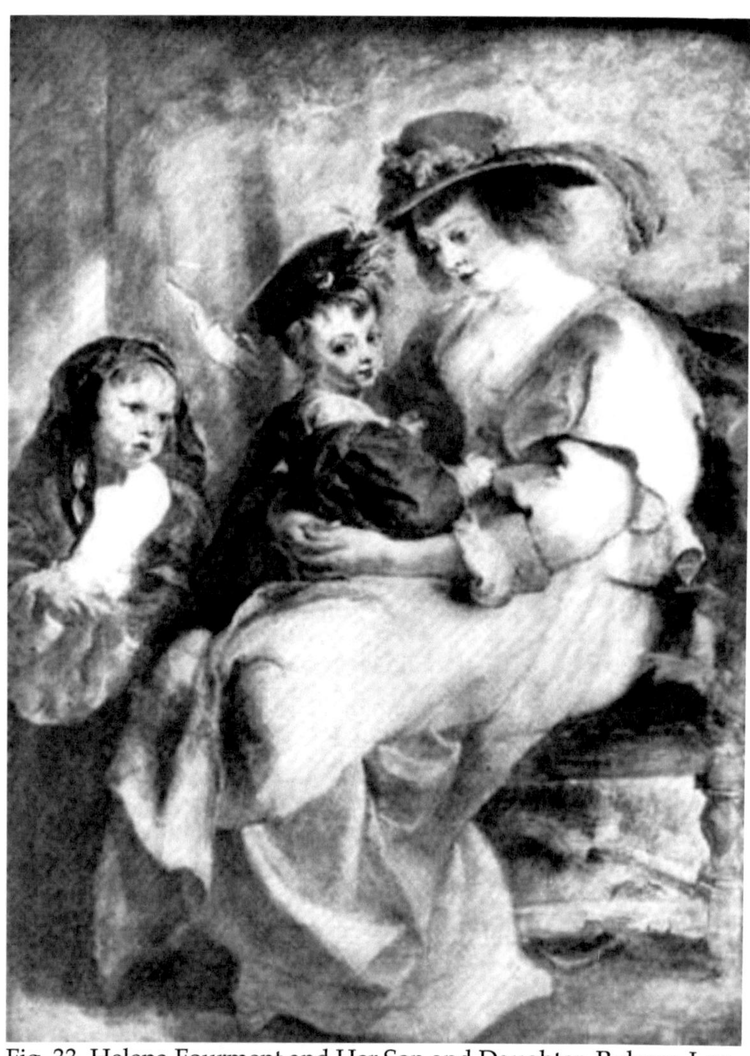

Fig. 33. Helena Fourment and Her Son and Daughter. Rubens. Louvre, Paris

[68]

THE HARP OF THE WINDS

Homer Martin (1836-1897)

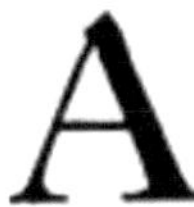

bout a dozen years ago Europe began to wonder if America had any art worth considering. She invited us to send samples of our paintings that her critics might judge of our work. Among the pictures selected was Homer Martin's "The Harp of the Winds." At once Europe saw that an American artist had painted a masterpiece.

This scene is on the River Seine, a short distance from Paris. Was anything ever more simple? Slender willow-trees almost leafless, bare rocks with a few scrubby bushes, a tiny village sheltered in a curve of the river—what is there to suggest a picture? And yet something grips us. We seem to be at the beginnings of creation. Nature is confiding in us. We are hearing the winds play on the harp to the listening river. See how lovingly the water mirrors those harp strings all sparkly with gold and green! I wonder if these willows make a harp or a lyre with their tall stalks reaching to the sky? Do you remember how, when Mercury found a tortoise, he took the shell and made holes on both sides and strung nine strings across it—one for each Muse—and gave it to Apollo? I think this Harp of the Winds has nine strings in memory of Mercury's lyre. [69]

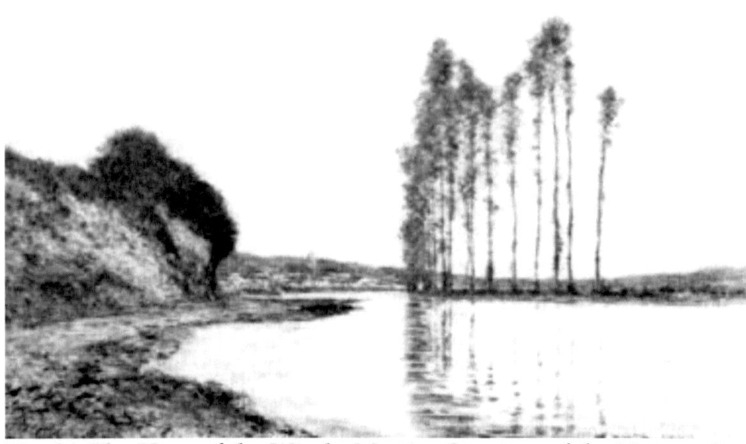

Fig. 34. The Harp of the Winds. Martin. Courtesy of the Metropolitan Museum of Art, New York City

[70]

THE TRIBUTE MONEY

Titian, or Tiziano Vecelli (1477-1576)

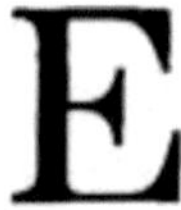

Every child must know "The Tribute Money," painted by Titian, for no artist understood the scene better than he did. Remember that the bad men in Palestine were determined to find something that Jesus, the Christ, had done against the Roman Government so they could trap him. At last they sent one in authority to question him.

But Jesus said, "Bring me a penny, that I may see it." And they brought him a penny.

And Jesus said, "Whose is this image and superscription?"

And the man was forced to say, "Cæsar's."

Then Jesus made that famous reply that people use so often to-day: "Render to Cæsar the things that are Cæsar's, and to God the things that are God's."

Titian shows the moment when the tax-gatherer must say that the penny belonged to Cæsar, the Roman emperor. It had Cæsar's portrait on it and Cæsar's demands written on it. Look carefully at the two faces and the two hands, and tell me what you think of the two men as Titian shows them to us. [71]

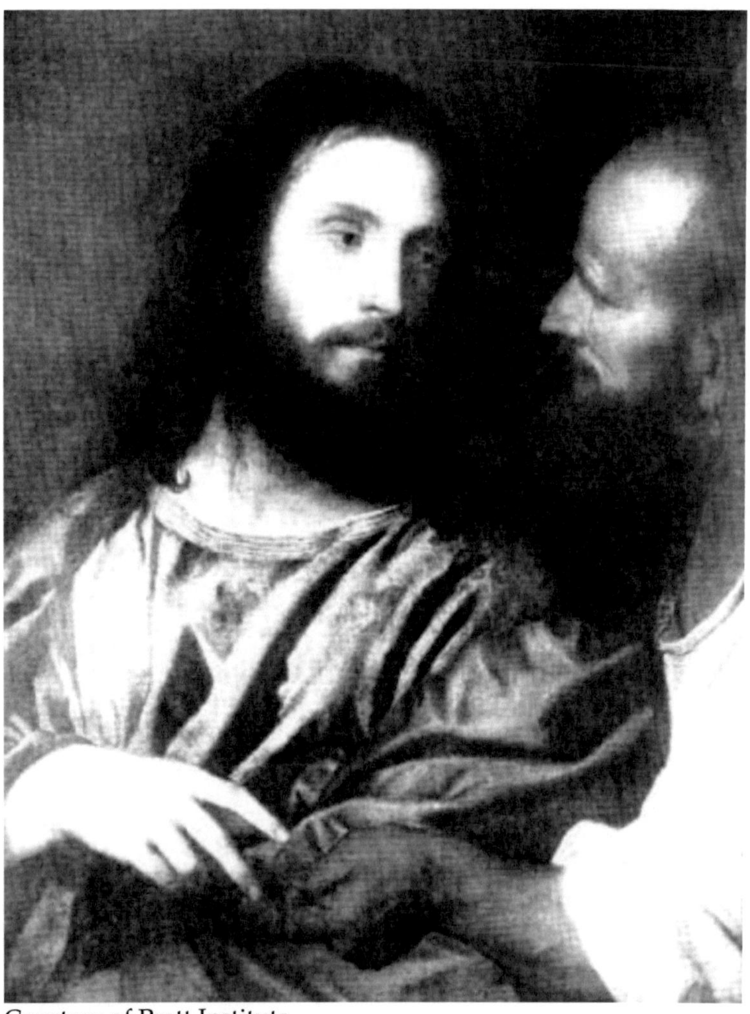

Courtesy of Pratt Institute

Fig. 35. The Tribute Money. Titian. Dresden Gallery

[72]

THE MAIDS OF HONOR

Diego Rodriguez de Silva y Velasquez (1599-1660)

If it had not been for Velasquez we should know very little about the little princes and princesses of Spain in the time of Philip IV, about the middle of the sixteenth century. He made many portraits of these children, especially of the little Princess Margarita.

One day when Velasquez was painting a portrait of Philip IV, the king's little daughter Margarita came into the room attended by her maids of honor and a splendid dog. The king was so delighted with the little group that he told Velasquez to make a picture of them just as they stood there before him. Now look at the picture and you will see in the looking-glass at the back of the room the reflection of the king and the queen. At the easel stands Velasquez, the artist, with his palette and brushes. The wee fair-haired princess is the center of the group. The strange-looking little women, her maids of honor, are dwarfs. And see what a magnificent fellow the dog is, lying so contentedly on the floor right in front of us.

When the picture was finished, and the people went to see it, many of them asked, "Where is the picture?" The little Margarita and her maids are so alive and those people standing around seem so real that no one thought they could be painted on canvas.

Velasquez made such wonderfully real likenesses that some one told this story of one: One day the King came to Velasquez's studio and seeing, as he supposed, one of his admirals whom he had sent to take a command a few days before, he spoke angrily:

"What! still here? Did I not command you to depart? Why have you not obeyed?" Of course the admiral did not answer, and then the king found that he had been angry at a portrait. [73]

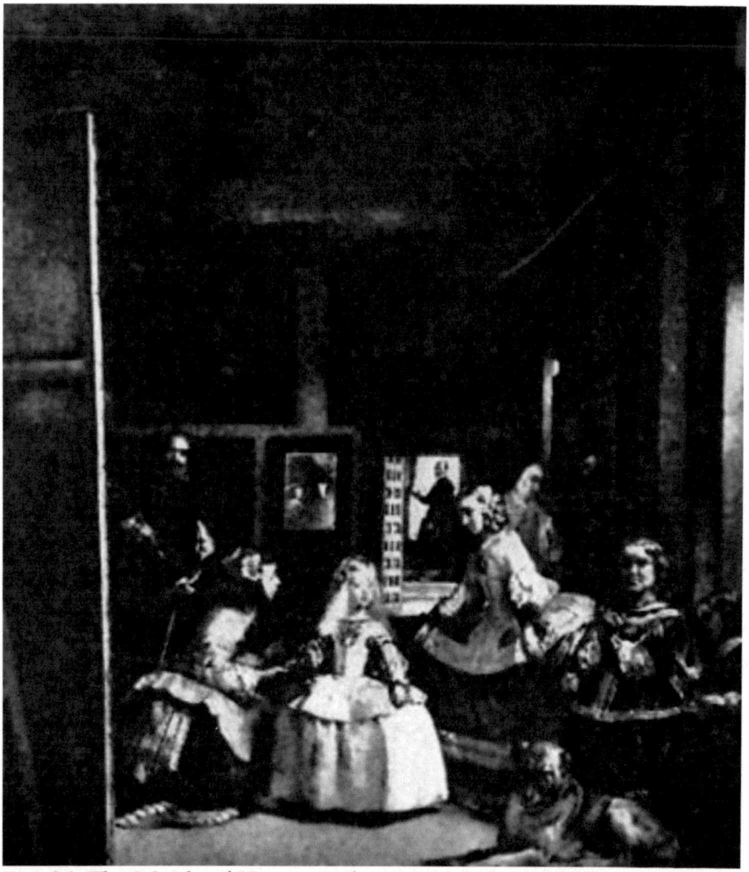

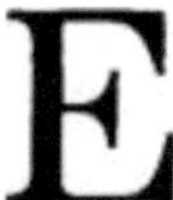

Fig. 36. The Maids of Honor. Velasquez. Madrid Gallery, Spain

[74]

THE NYMPHS

Jean Baptiste Camille Corot (1796-1875)

E

verybody loved Père Corot—Papa Corot, as he was called. His happy manner and lovely smile won for him the name of the "happy one." I want you to know what Papa Corot says, in a letter to a friend, about himself and his painting. He writes:

"Look you, it is charming, the day of a landscapist. He gets up at three in the morning, before sunrise, goes and sits under a tree, and watches and waits. Not much can be seen at first. Nature is behind a veil. Everything smells sweet.

"Ping! a ray of yellow light shoots up. The veil is torn, and meadow and valley and hill are peeping through the rent.

"Bing, bing! the sun's first ray—another ray—and the flowers awake and drink a drop of quivering dew. The leaves feel cold and move to and fro. Under the leaves unseen birds are singing softly. The flowers are saying their morning prayers.

"Bam! the sun has risen. Bam! a peasant crosses the field with a cart and oxen. Ding! ding! says the bell of the ram that leads the flock of sheep.

"Bam! bam! all bursts—all glitters—all is full of light, blond and caressing as yet. The flowers raise their heads. It is adorable. I paint! I paint!

"Boom! boom! boom! The sun aflame burns the earth. Everything becomes heavy. Let us go home. We see too much now. Let us go home."

You see now why Corot could paint such a lovely picture as "The Nymphs." He saw these gauzy creatures in the early morning light and painted them before the sun scattered them to the four winds. [75]

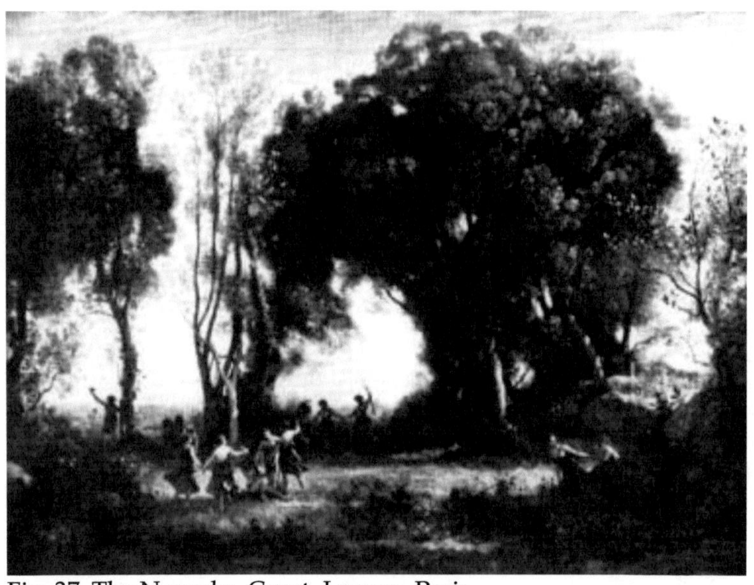

Fig. 37. The Nymphs. Corot. Louvre, Paris

[76]

ST. FRANCIS PREACHING TO THE BIRDS

Giotto di Bondone (1266?-1337)

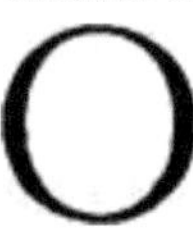

ne time more than six hundred years ago St. Francis preached the dearest sermon to "My Sisters the Birds" that you ever heard. He said to them as they lifted their little heads to listen to his words:

"Ye are beholden unto God your Creator, and always and in every place it is your duty to praise him! Ye are bounden to him for the element of the air which he has deputed to you forever-more. You sow not, neither do you reap. God feeds you and gives you the streams and fountains for your thirst. He gives you the mountains and the valleys for your refuge, tall trees wherein to make your nests, and inasmuch as you neither spin nor reap God clothes you and your children, hence ye should love your Creator greatly, and therefore beware, my sisters, of the sins of ingratitude, and ever strive to praise God."

St. Francis then made the sign of the Cross and sent the birds north, south, east, and west to carry the story of the Cross to all mankind.

When Giotto, who painted this picture of "St. Francis Preaching to the Birds," was a little boy, he took care of his father's sheep in the fields. One day a noted painter, Cimabue, found Giotto drawing a sheep on a flat rock with colored stones. The picture of the sheep was so lifelike that the great man asked the boy, Giotto, to go with him and become an artist. He went, and one day years afterward the pope sent to Giotto for a sample of his work. Giotto sent him a big round O. It pleased the pope to find a man so original, and he gave Giotto many orders for pictures. To-day the saying is "Round as Giotto's O." [77]

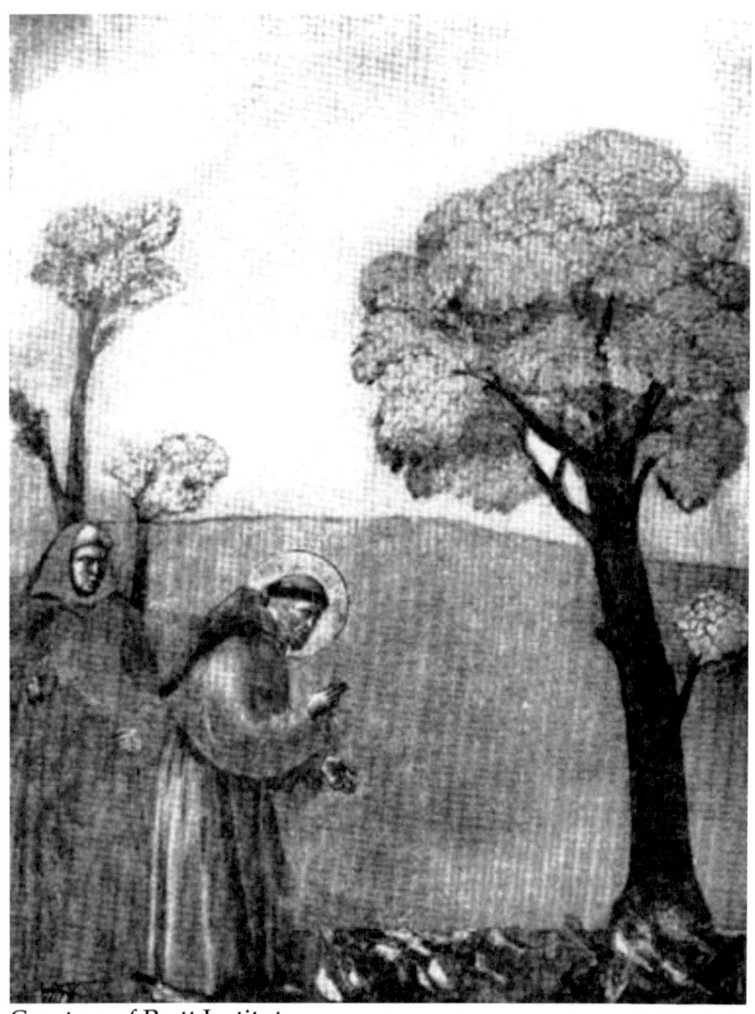

Courtesy of Pratt Institute

Fig. 38. St. Francis Preaching to the Birds. Giotto. Upper Church, Assisi, Italy

[78]

THE GOVERNESS

Jean Baptiste Simeon Chardin (1699-1779)

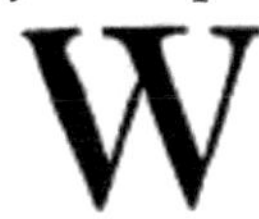

When Chardin began to paint pictures he went into the French homes and painted pictures of brass pots and kettles, of fruits and vegetables. Then he took common scenes of life and gave us a number of pictures showing just what was going on in the homes and back yards.

The French people were not used to having an artist see beauty in the every-day things they were doing; artists had been painting the rich for the rich. Everybody began to love the pictures Chardin painted. This is a very simple story in "The Governess." The child—is it a boy or a girl?—is now ready to go to school. He—I believe he is a boy—is hearing some advice, and I do not think he is pleased, for he has a little frown on his face. His dress is peculiar. The French children two hundred years ago did not dress as you do to-day. He is the same kind of a child that you are, I am sure, and you and he would soon be great friends.

Chardin's color was so wonderful that one of his artist friends cried out: "O Chardin! it is not white, red, or black that you grind to powder on your palette; it is the air and the light that you take on the point of your brush and fix on canvas."

Chardin's pictures are as beautiful and bright to-day as they were when he painted them. [79]

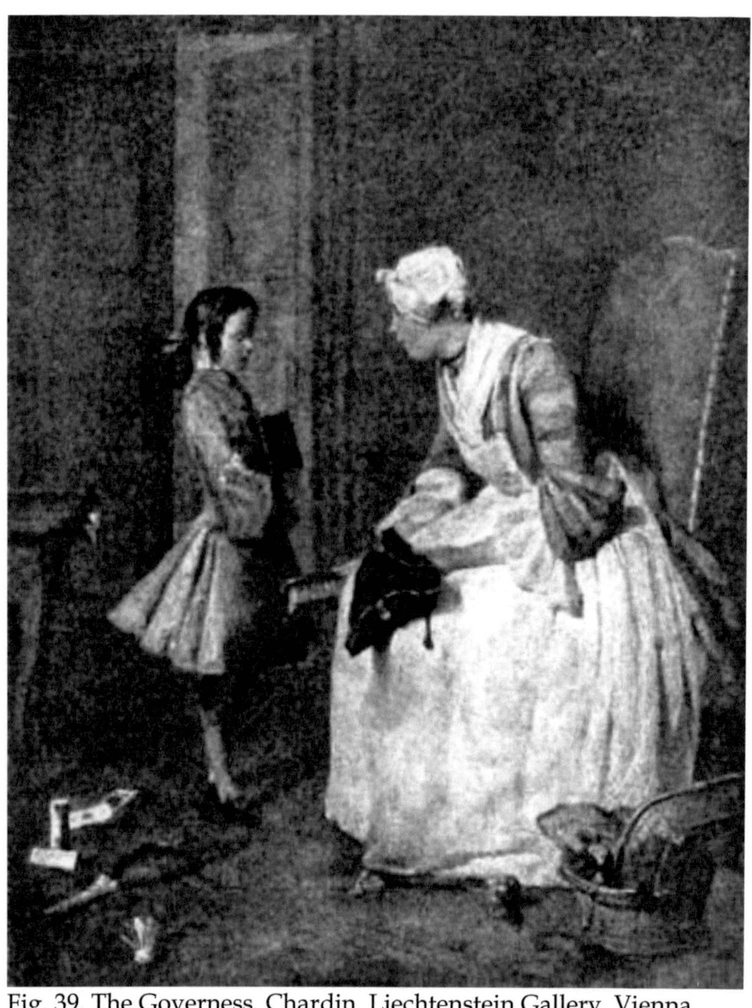

Fig. 39. The Governess. Chardin. Liechtenstein Gallery, Vienna
[80]

THE LAST SUPPER

Leonardo da Vinci (1452-1519)

I want you to know the disciples of Jesus just as Leonardo da Vinci painted them four hundred years ago. Leonardo spent months among the men of Milan, Italy, looking into their faces and talking with them. When he began to paint "The Last Supper" he had gathered men together so like these twelve disciples that we feel we can know them as Jesus knew them. For three years those men of old walked with Jesus and talked with him as they went up and down Palestine; and at last, on that wonderful night, they met with Him in the upper chamber to eat with Him the Last Supper. Those disciples did not know that it was the last meal they would eat with Jesus before he was hung on the cross.

We shall begin in the center of the table and name the disciples as Leonardo has them in the picture. First is the Savior. At his left is James with his arms spread out in distress; back of him is Thomas with his finger uplifted; then Philip rising with his hand on his heart; next Matthew, his arms pointing to the Savior while he turns toward the two near the end; next to him is Thaddeus; and then Simon. On the other side of Jesus sits John, the beloved disciple. His hands are folded and his eyes are cast down. Next to John is Judas, the betrayer; he holds the bag clutched in his right hand and near him is the overturned salt cellar. Leaning back of Judas is Peter with one hand on John's shoulder; next to Peter is Andrew; then James, the less, laying one hand on Peter's arm. At the end of the table is Bartholomew, who has risen resting his hands on the table. These men are all asking, "Is it I?" For Jesus had said, "He it is to whom I give a sop." [81]

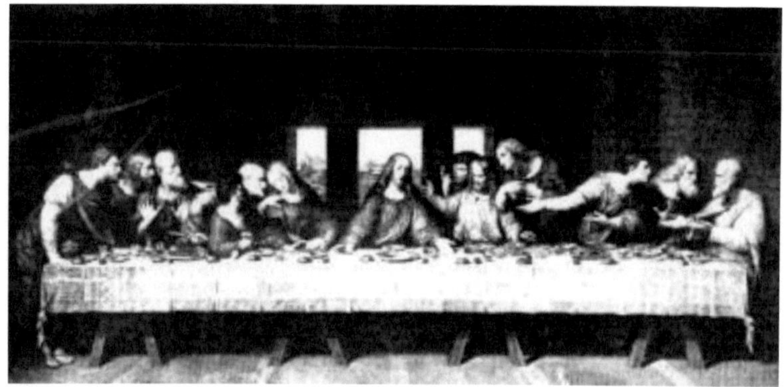

Fig. 40. The Last Supper. Leonardo da Vinci. Santa Maria delle Grazie, Milan

[82]

SIR GALAHAD

George Frederick Watts (1818-1904)

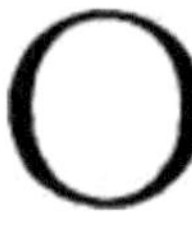

O f all the stories of King Arthur and his Knights of the Round Table none is so strange as that of Sir Galahad. Its beginning is in the upper chamber at the Last Supper with Jesus and his disciples. Legend says that the cup used by our Savior at the Last Supper was the Holy Grail. Joseph of Arimathea, who bought the cup from Pontius Pilate, used it to catch the blood that flowed from the pierced side of our Lord. The cup, or Holy Grail, was kept in the Convent of the Holy Grail by the descendants of Joseph of Arimathea.

The cup had marvelous powers in the hands of a perfect knight. Centuries passed and no perfect knight came to claim the Holy Grail. Then King Arthur founded the Knights of the Round Table. One seat at the round table was always vacant waiting for the sinless youth. Many tried to sit in the "seat perilous," as it was called, but the seat let each one down to disappear forever.

At last an old man—Joseph of Arimathea himself—brought a boy and seated him in the vacant chair. The knights were frightened but the boy sat unharmed and above the seat appeared the words:

THIS IS THE SEAT OF GALAHAD

King Arthur knighted him and sent him forth to find the Holy Grail. Years went by and awful trials and temptations came to Sir Galahad. He did not yield to the bad things that came, but kept looking for the Holy Grail. At last he held the cross before his face to keep off his tormentors when before his eyes he saw the cup, and the power of the Holy Grail came to him.

This picture of Sir Galahad in Eton College, England, hangs in the chapel opposite the entrance door where each boy passes in on his way to morning and evening prayers. [83]

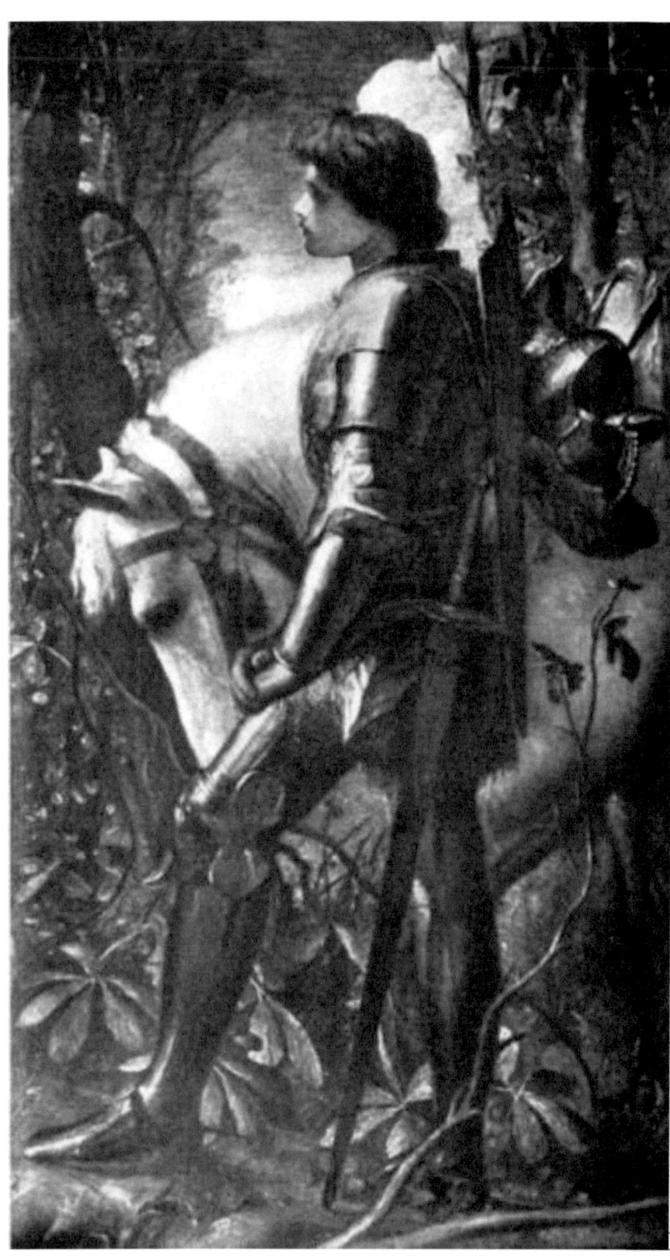

Fig. 41.

[84]

THE DUCHESS OF DEVONSHIRE AND HER CHILD

Sir Joshua Reynolds (1723-1792)

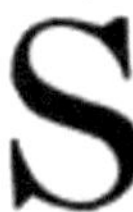ir Joshua Reynolds ought to be called "the painter of little girls." No artist ever painted a larger number of little girls. And no artist ever knew better than he how to get the confidence of children, boys or girls.

One time a little boy in London was to carry a flag in a procession. What do you think he did? He went to Sir Joshua Reynolds, the artist whom no one dared to interrupt, and asked him if he would paint a flag for him. This pleased the great man. When the boy proudly displayed his flag, every one asked:

"Where did you get such a wonderful flag?"

You can guess how proud the boy was to say, "Sir Joshua Reynolds painted it for me!"

This picture of "The Duchess of Devonshire and her Child" is one of the greatest pictures Sir Joshua ever painted. The original painting is now in the magnificent country seat of the Duke of Devonshire at Chatsworth, England. Sir Joshua had a way of making his pictures sparkle and glisten that was unknown to other artists. One of our own artists, Gilbert Stuart, when in London, was copying a very valuable portrait by Sir Joshua. He thought he saw one of the eyes move. He was horrified to find that it really was moving down on the cheek. He grabbed the picture and ran into a cold room and then worked the eye back in place. The secret was out! Sir Joshua Reynolds had used wax to make his pictures glitter and, alas, the glitter would not last. [85]

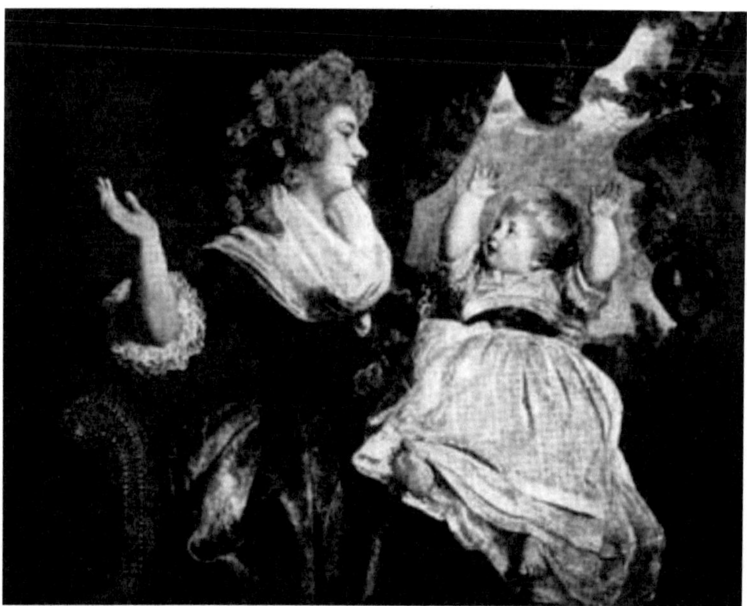

Fig. 42. The Duchess of Devonshire and Her Child. Reynolds. Royal Gallery, Windsor

[86]

ST. AGNES AND HER LAMB

Andrea del Sarto (1486-1531)

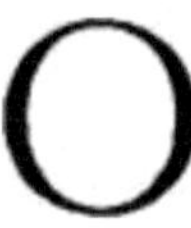

One of the most beautiful pictures of "St. Agnes and her lamb" was painted by Andrea del Sarto,—"Andrea the faultless," as he was called. It is in the cathedral at Pisa.

St. Agnes was a Roman girl who lived three hundred years after the birth of Jesus. Her father and mother were heathens, but their little daughter became a Christian when a mere child. She did not tell her parents that she loved Jesus, but when she refused to worship idols they knew that she had become a disciple of the Master

Christ. This made them so angry that they handed her over to the Roman rulers to be punished. These wicked men tried in every way to persuade Agnes to bow down to their gods made of wood and stone. When she would not bow down to them they tried to force her to worship the idols.

They gave her over to the soldiers and ordered them to take her clothes away, but immediately her hair grew and covered her, and angels came and gave her a shining white garment. She even refused to marry the son of the Roman magistrate. The son thought that he could compel her to consent to the marriage after she was persecuted, but he was struck blind when he tried to see her.

When St. Agnes saw what great sorrow came to the home of the young nobleman because he was blind, she prayed for him and his eyesight came again. His father was so thankful that he pleaded for her life, but the people said,

"She is a sorceress: she must die." Then they tried to burn her, but the flames burned her tormentors and did her no harm. At last she was killed with a sword. She is always represented with a lamb.

Michael Angelo wrote to Raphael about Andrea del Sarto: "There is a little fellow in Florence who, if he were employed as you are upon great works, would make it hot for you." [87]

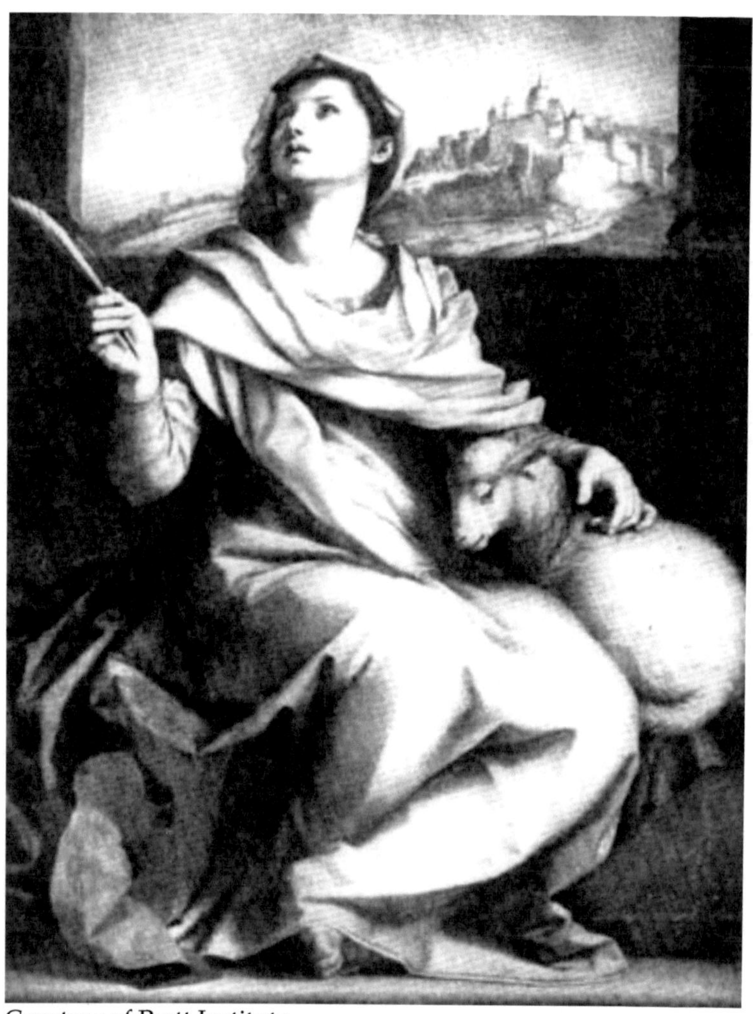

Courtesy of Pratt Institute

Fig. 43. St. Agnes and Her Lamb. Andrea del Sarto. Pisa Cathedral, Italy

[88]

WHISTLER'S MOTHER

James Abbott McNeill Whistler (1834-1903)

The story about Whistler and his mother is rather a sad one. He went to Europe when he was a young painter and told his mother as he started that he would come home to her when he had made a success. But he never made a success in money. He painted this picture of his mother and for twenty years tried to sell it. He offered it to his own country—the United States—for five hundred dollars. We were so stupid that we did not know that the picture was a masterpiece and that no amount of money could buy it later on. But the people of Paris began to feel that Whistler, the American artist, was a great master, and the city bought the picture, "Whistler's Mother." Of course we can never own the picture now, although it is an American mother, unless the French people should give it to us. But we do not deserve it, do we?

After a number of years Whistler's mother went to Europe to make a home for her wonderful son. She died in Chelsea, and to-day the mother and son are side by side in the little churchyard of Chiswick, near London. [89]

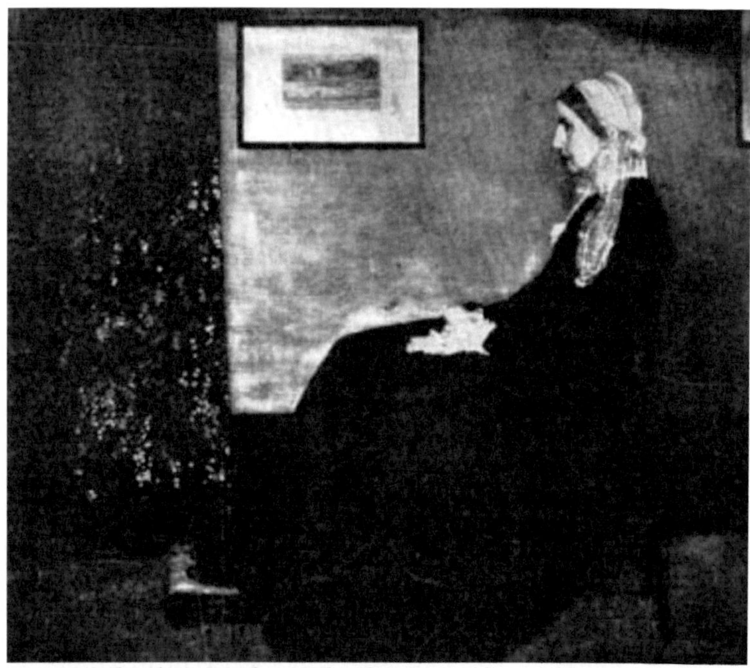

Fig. 44. Whistler's Mother. Whistler. Luxembourg, Paris

[90]

ST. CHRISTOPHER

Titian, or Tiziano Vecelli (1477-1576)

C

hristopher, or Offero, was born in Palestine in the third century. He was a giant in size but ignorant and poor. He felt that he could not work for any one who was afraid of any one else. He wandered over the country and at last he came to a powerful king and offered to work for him. The king thought it very fine to have a giant for a servant. One day Offero stood by the king's side while a minstrel sang a song about Satan. Every time the name of Satan was spoken

90

the king crossed himself. Offero was puzzled, for he never had heard of Satan, nor of Jesus. When he found that the king was afraid of Satan, Offero went to find the man the king was afraid of.

Offero found Satan and became his servant. But as they went through the land Offero saw that Satan always went away around the little shrines. Offero asked Satan why he did that. Satan said he did not like to come near the cross where was the crucified One. Then Offero knew that he was afraid of Jesus.

He went out to find Jesus. At last an old hermit told Offero to go to a river where people were often drowned and to carry every one across on his back, and that maybe he would find Jesus. Offero built himself a hut and spent years carrying people over the stream and no one was drowned. One stormy night Offero thought he heard a child's voice calling him. He went out two or three times. At last the child appeared and asked Offero to carry him over. Offero started. The storm grew worse and the water rose high and the child grew very, very heavy. When Offero set the child down, he said, "I feel as though I had carried the whole world!" The child answered:

"Offero, you have carried the maker of the world. I am Jesus, whom you have sought. You shall be called Christ-Offero—the Christ-bearer—from now on." [91]

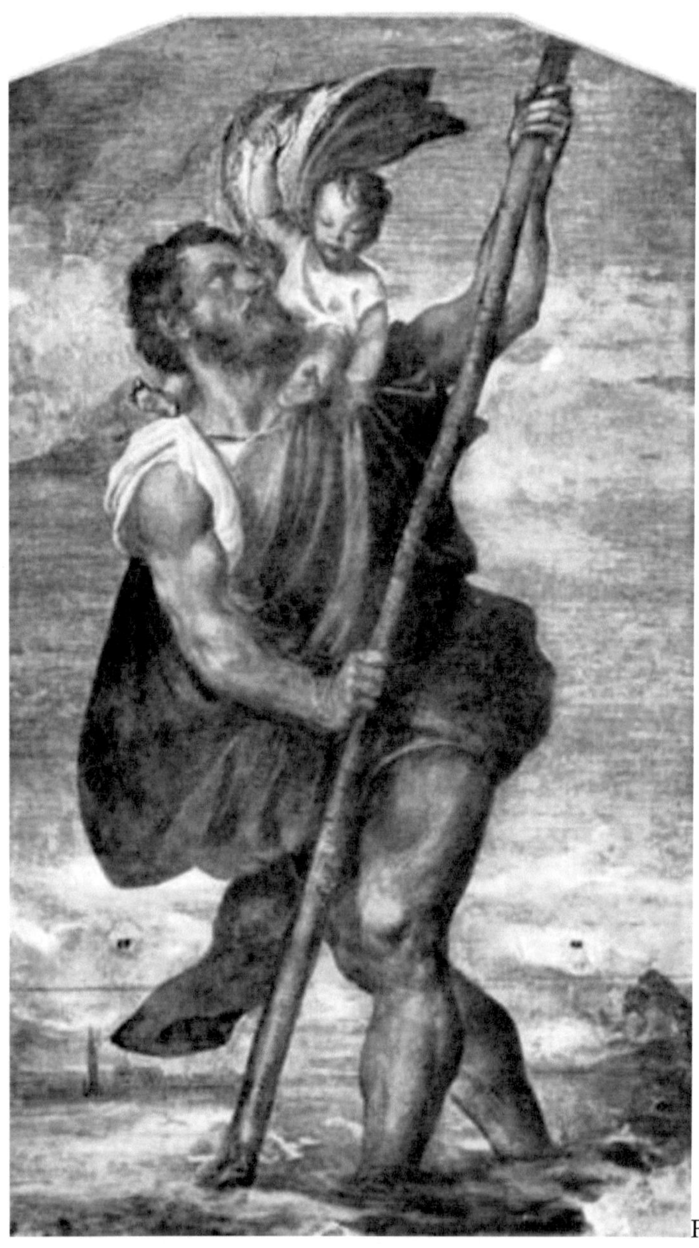

Fig.

45. St. Christopher. Titian. Doges' Palace, Venice

[92]

THE BLUE BOY

Thomas Gainsborough (1727-1788)

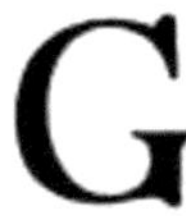

ainsborough began to draw and paint when he was a child. He often entertained his companions by drawing pictures for them while they read the lessons to him.

One morning Thomas got up with the sun and went out into the garden to sketch. There was in the garden a wonderful pear-tree full of ripe pears, and the pears had been disappearing very mysteriously. While Thomas was making his drawings he saw a man's face appear suddenly above the stone wall. He quickly made a sketch of the face, and frightened the man before he could get away with the fruit. At the breakfast-table the young artist told his father what he had done and showed him the sketch. His father knew the man and sent for him. When the man was accused of stealing the pears he denied it, but when he was shown the picture Thomas had made of him he confessed that he had taken the pears.

Artists, like all of us, want to lay down rules for every one to follow who is doing their same kind of work. Sir Joshua Reynolds said, "The masses of light in a picture ought to be always of a warm, mellow colour—yellow, red, or yellowish white; and the blue, the grey, or green colours should be kept almost entirely out of the masses." Gainsborough did not agree with him. To show Sir Joshua that he was wrong Gainsborough painted pictures in blue and green. The famous "Blue Boy" alone proved that he was right. The boy has on a blue satin suit and he stands out-of-doors in green grass with green foliage and blue sky around him. When Sir Joshua saw Gainsborough's blue-green pictures he said frankly, "I cannot think how he produces his effects."

These two men were never good friends yet when Gainsborough was near death Sir Joshua Reynolds came to his bedside, and when Gainsborough died Reynolds was one of the pall-bearers. [93]

94

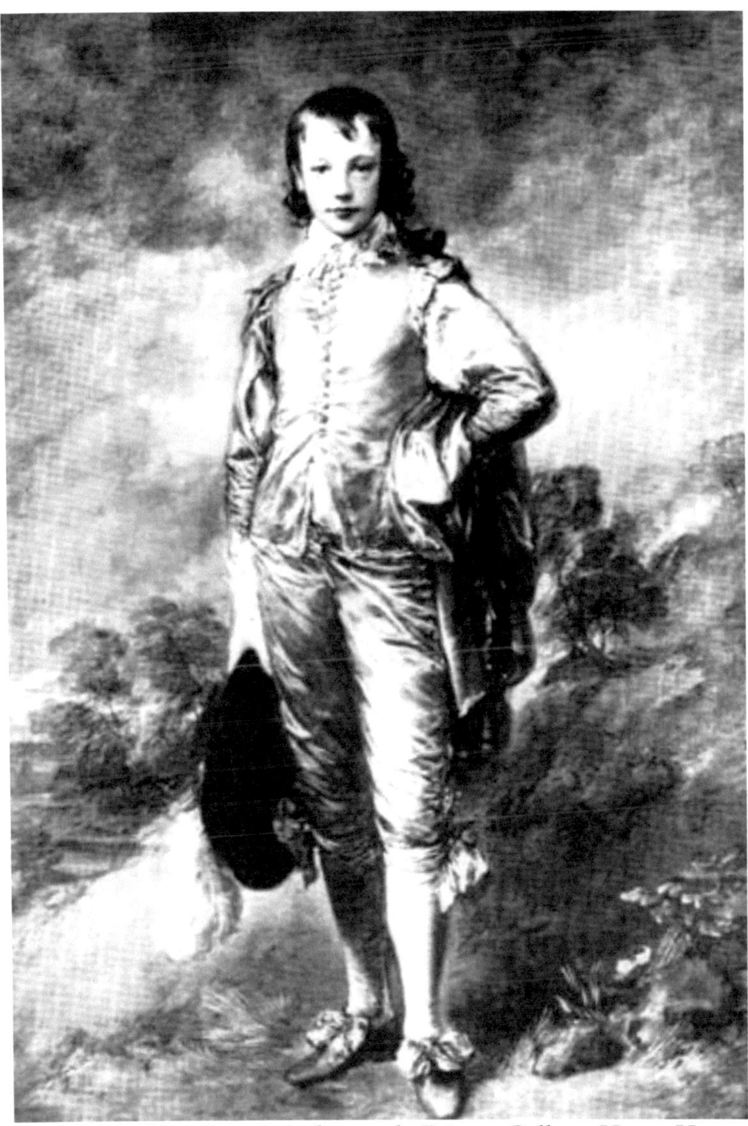

Fig. 46. The Blue Boy. Gainsborough. Private Gallery, Henry Huntington, Los Angeles, California

[94]

THE SLEEPING GIRL

Jan van der Meer of Delft (1632-1675)

I want you to know and love the Dutch pictures. The painters were called "little masters," simply because they painted small pictures for the homes. For the homes! The Dutch wanted pictures to hang on their walls; pictures they could live with. Now what do you think of the "Sleeping Girl"? Do you know I could live with that picture and feel that I always had something to make me happy? It is so homy. See how comfortable the girl is! Of course a good healthy girl has no business to be sleeping in the daytime, but we can forgive her now that van der Meer has caught her asleep and let us see her. Then look at that wonderful rug! Was ever anything so soft and velvety? If we knew about rugs we might tell its name and maybe its age.

Van der Meer had a way of catching people without their knowing it. He seems to have cut a piece out of the wall where he peeped in and painted what he saw. We are glad the girl left the door open into another room so that we can see the table and pictures and part of the window-frame. I think these things are reflected in a looking-glass.

Van der Meer painted only about forty pictures, and eight of those are in the United States. They are among our greatest art treasures. [95]

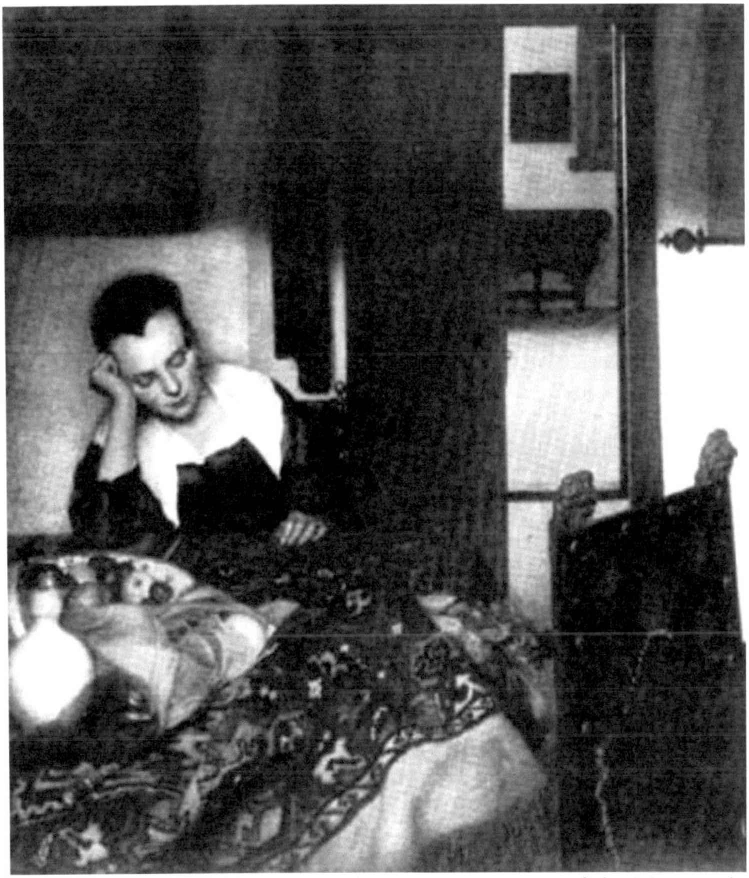

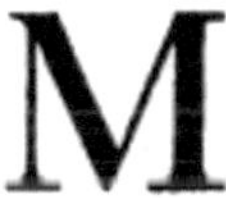

Fig. 47. The Sleeping Girl. Van der Meer. Courtesy of the Metropolitan Museum of Art, New York City

[96]

ST. ANTONY AND THE CHRIST-CHILD

Bartholome Esteban Murillo (1618-1682)

M

any very curious legends are told of St. Antony of Padua, who died in 1231. He was a close friend of St. Francis (see "St. Francis and his Birds," page 76). One story says that one time he was preaching about the Savior when the child Jesus came and sat on his open Bible. It is this story that Murillo painted his picture to illustrate. Again and again Murillo has shown us St. Antony with the Christ-child, but never more beautifully than here. This is one of Murillo's greatest religious pictures.

Another story is told of St. Antony. One day he was preaching the funeral sermon of a rich young man when he exclaimed:

"His heart is buried in his treasure-chest; go seek it there and you will find it."

Sure enough when the friends of the rich young man opened the treasure-chest there was the heart, and no heart was found in the young man's dead body. [97]

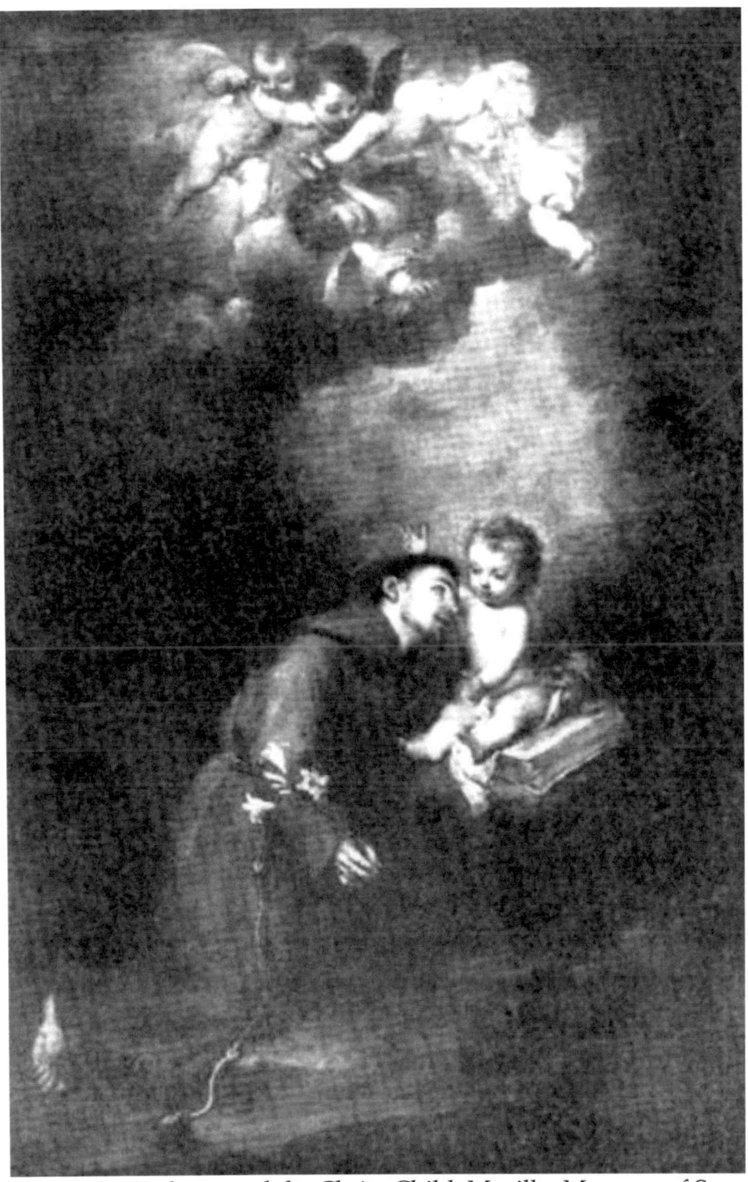

Fig. 48. St. Anthony and the Christ-Child. Murillo. Museum of Seville, Spain.

[98]

KING LEAR

Edwin Austin Abbey (1852-1911)

The story of "King Lear" is one of the most pitiful of Shakespeare's play. It is about the thanklessness of children to a father. Old *King Lear* had three daughters—*Goneril, Regan,* and *Cordelia.* He loved these daughters dearly and he believed that they loved him. As he grew old in life he thought he would divide his kingdom and property among them equally; then there would be no trouble about his wealth after he was dead. Of course he expected to make his home with them in turn as long as he lived. Naturally he went to *Goneril,* the eldest daughter, first. Very soon he found that he was not wanted. She had the money—her father's money—but why should she be troubled with her old father? He then went to *Regan,* his second child, but she too refused to make a home for him. The third daughter, *Cordelia,* loved her father dearly and wanted him to live with her that she might care for him in his old age. By a strange mishap the old father thought that *Cordelia,* his beloved child, was false to him. He wandered off on the heath in a fearful storm and at last found shelter in a hut where he thinks even his faithful dogs are against him. He cries out pitifully:

> The little dogs and all,
> Tray, Blanche and Sweetheart, see they bark at me.

Abbey has painted the scene when the old king is leaving heartbroken, for he thinks *Cordelia,* the child he loves best, is deserting him. *Cordelia,* knowing how false her sisters are, is saying:

> I know you what you are;
> And, like a sister, am most loath to call

100

Your faults as they are named. Love well our father.

Abbey's story of "The Holy Grail" in the Boston Library is one of America's great series of paintings for wall decoration. [99]

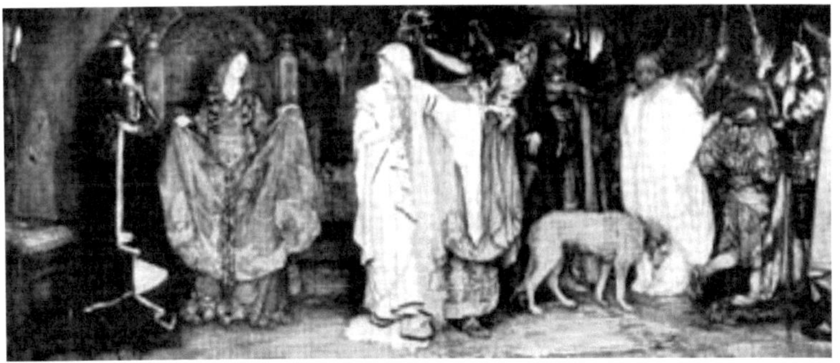

Fig. 49. King Lear. Abbey. Courtesy of the Metropolitan Museum of Art, New York City.

[100]

SUNSET IN THE WOODS

George Inness (1825-1894)

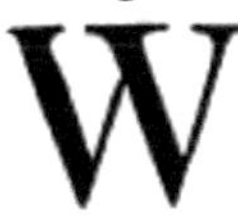

henever you can, I want you to find out what the painter says about his own pictures. We feel very glad that George Inness told us about "Sunset in the Woods." He said in 1891: "The material for my picture was taken from a sketch made near Hastings, on the Hudson, New York, twenty years ago. This picture was commenced seven years ago, but until last winter I had not obtained any idea equal to the impression received on the spot. The idea is to express an effect of light in the woods at sunset."

What a wonderful glow he has on those trees beyond the big rock away back in the picture. And see the light on the trunk of the big tree near us. I believe the light is gradually disappearing as we look. Somehow we feel the birds are twittering as they go to bed and the flowers are nodding their heads, they are so sleepy. Soon it will be dark and the owl will screech and the night insects will buzz. Come, we must go home or we cannot see our way! [101]

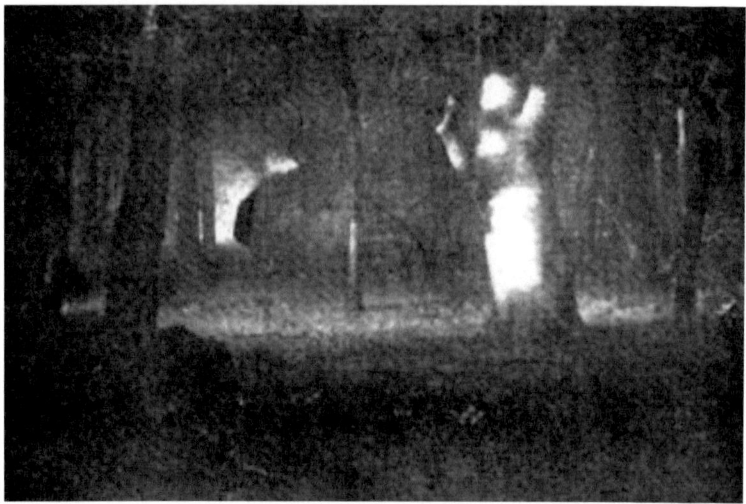

Fig. 50. Sunset in the Woods. Inness. Courtesy of the Corcoran Art Gallery, Washington, D. C.

[103]